THE HISTORY OF THE ATCHISON, TOPEKA &
Santa Fe

THE HISTORY OF THE ATCHISON, TOPEKA &
Santa Fe

Edited by
Pamela Berkman

Bonanza
A Bison Book

Published 1988 by
Bonanza Books, distributed by
Crown Publishers Inc

Produced by Bison Books Corp
15 Sherwood Place
Greenwich, CT 06830, USA

Printed in Hong Kong

ISBN 0-517-63350-7
h g f e d c b

Designed by Ruth DeJauregui
Captioned by Timothy Jacobs

Acknowledgements

The editor would like to acknowledge the help of those parties who supplied materials without which this book would not have been possible: Santa Fe Industries; The Atchison, Topeka & Santa Fe Railway; Amfac, Inc; and the Fred Harvey Company whose press materials have been adapted for part of this text. Also indispensible from a reference point of view were the excellent sources of information *Santa Fe, the Railroad that Built an Empire*, by James Marshall and *History of the Atchison, Topeka & Santa Fe Railway* by Keith L Bryant, Jr.

Photo Credits
All photos courtesy of the **Santa Fe Southern Pacific Corporation** except:
AGS Archives: 54
Amtrak: 67 (bottom right)
Bancroft Library, University of California at Berkeley: 26, 30–31
HL Broadbelt: 90–91 (bottom)
Denver & Rio Grande Western Railroad: 18–19
Nils Huxtable, Steamscenes: 23, 101, 108, (top), 109, 117, 125

McDonnell Douglas: 86, 88–89 (bottom)
Seaver Center for Western History Research, Natural History Museum of Los Angeles County: 45, 21, 58–59, 62–63 (right), 64, 69
University of Arizona Library: 38–39, 42, 44 (top), 45, 46–47 (bottom), 48, 61, 66 (right), 75, 88 (top)
© **Bill Yenne**: 68

Page 1: The Santa Fe's famous *Super Chief* negotiates a serpentine stretch of track en route from Los Angeles to Chicago, near Lamy, New Mexico. Amtrak has since taken over the bulk of passenger service for US railroads.

Pages 2–3: Near Hesperia, California, two modern road switchers give an assist to a Santa Fe freight train—by way of pushing from the rear—on the east side grade of Cajon Pass.

These pages: At right in this turn-of-the-century photo is a rear view of the old Santa Fe station in Los Angeles. Note the old-style cars on the tracks, and the streetcar on the elevated roadway at photo left.

Contents

In the Beginning

The Old Santa Fe Trail

The mere mention of Santa Fe is sufficient to conjure up images of a railroad. Bright red and yellow diesels followed by gleaming stainless steel passenger coaches and long freight trains thundering across the plains through waving wheat fields. How did this empire begin?

At one end there was Independence, Missouri. At the other rested Santa Fe, an exotic city nestling in the remoteness of the 'Great American Desert.' Between the two lay some 800 miles of faintly marked trail, snaking its way across the plains and through the mountains. This barely visible thoroughfare was destined to become a major artery of commerce.

Before Mexico received its independence from Spain, traders from United States outposts to the east were met with a notable lack of enthusiasm upon arrival at Santa Fe. The ruling Spaniards discouraged such trade by the simple and excellent expedient of jailing unsuspecting traders and confiscating their merchandise.

The first successful attempt to carry on overland trade with Santa Fe was a small expedition from Missouri organized and led by Captain William Becknell in 1821, shortly after Mexico gained its freedom. So successful was Becknell's first trip that a larger expedition was formed the next year, and a new and shorter route to Santa Fe was pioneered and mapped.

Both routes departed southwesterly from Council Grove, Kansas, and intersected the Arkansas River near Great Bend, following the river to a point just east of Dodge City. Here the trails diverged, one branch heading generally south and west across the plains to Las Vegas, and the other, more generally used, followed the Arkansas River to La Junta and turned south over the Raton Pass to Las Vegas. Both of these routes are roughly the same as those followed by the Santa Fe Railroad of today. After Becknell's second caravan, commerce over the Santa Fe Trail expanded by leaps and bounds.

Thus, from its very beginning the trail was a two-way road of trade—a highway traversed by strings of laden pack mules. This limited form of transport was soon replaced by lengthy wagon trains inching westward with bulging loads of various trade goods from the more heavily settled East. On the return trip, wagon wheels squealed under their huge cargoes of furs and precious metals from the Mexican mines.

As trade expanded and navigation of the Missouri River extended westward, so too, the outfitting points for the caravans moved further west to Kansas City and Independence. Normal practice was for the adventurous trader to

The visionary Cyrus Kurtz Holliday *(at right)* is known as the father of the Santa Fe Railroad. The Atchison and Topeka Railroad—the foundation of the Santa Fe system—was organized in September of 1860 in Luther Challis' Atchison, Kansas office which is shown *above.*

load his provisions and trade goods and strike out alone for Council Grove, a rendezvous point on the route to Santa Fe. At that point, for reasons of safety, wagon trains were formed and generally reached the profitable marketplace at Santa Fe in 80 or 90 days.

It was in full recognition of this ever-increasing commerce that the soon-to-be railroad builders, mindful of the tremendous potential, cast longing glances in the direction of Santa Fe.

Cyrus Holliday

Cyrus Kurtz Holliday was the father of the Santa Fe Railroad. He was a dreamer but also a doer—possessed of an engaging personality, imagination, resourcefulness and unlimited perseverance. Without all of these qualities, the tasks he set himself to would have been beyond accomplishment.

Holliday arrived on the Kansas scene during the fall of 1854 with two objectives in mind. He wanted to found a town in the new territory. However, even more important was his determination to build a railroad capable of transporting the vast amount of goods moving to and from the trappers and traders at Santa Fe—the trade center of the vast Southwest.

During his first few years in Kansas, he devoted all of his boundless energies to the establishment and promotion of the city of Topeka. He was largely responsible for its having been named the state capital in 1859. Having successfully accomplished the first of his two objectives, he became obsessed with the second of his dreams—building a railroad over the old Santa Fe Trail from the Missouri River to Santa Fe.

In the fall of 1857, Holliday had become acquainted with Luther C Challis, a pioneer merchant, banker and ferry operator of Atchison. Both were at the time members of the Kansas Territorial Legislature at Lawrence. They discussed the possible construction of a railroad between Topeka and Atchison.

The charter for the Atchison and Topeka Railroad—the base from which its present system grew—was prepared single-handedly by Holliday in a hotel room in Lawrence in 1859. As a member of the Territorial Legislature, Holliday introduced the charter on 1 February 1859. With the 'skids greased' by his foresight and advance groundwork, the bill sailed through both the House and Senate and was approved by the Governor on February 11.

The Civil War and the disarranged business conditions of the country made the raising of investment capital a lengthy and heartbreaking task, a struggle that endured for 10 years.

Nevertheless, the company was organized from September 15 to 17 in 1860, in the Atchison office of Luther Challis. Besides Holliday and Challis, participating were Peter T Abell, Asaph Allen, Lorenzo D Bird, F L Crane, Milton C Dickey, Samuel Dickson, George Fairchild, Wilson L Gordon, George S Hillyer, Jeremiah Murphy and Samuel C Pomeroy. The first board of directors and officers was elected on the 17th, with Holliday as president, Abell as secretary and Dickey as treasurer.

On 3 March 1863, a territorial law setting aside 2,931,247.54 acres for the company, dependent on construction of a railroad, was passed. Congress put one major stipulation on the land grants, however—that the Santa Fe would have to reach the Colorado border within 10 years to take title to the lands that were granted them. Then, on 7 August 1868, the company was legally authorized to buy 114,401.76 acres of the Pottawatomie Indian Reservation in eastern Kansas from the Leavenworth, Lawrence & Galveston Railroad. The land was purchased for $1 per acre and was to be resold to provide funds for construction, and also to be used as collateral for construction loans.

It was 30 October 1868 that saw the real beginning of the railroad—the turning of the first spade of earth at Topeka, near the bank of the Kaw River. The first construction was a pile bridge across the Kaw, connecting with the Kansas Pacific Railroad. The first station on the line was at Pauline, six miles south of and 243 feet above the starting point. Holliday took the occasion of the ground breaking to forecast again that the line would eventually extend to the city of Santa Fe. Carried away by his own enthusiasm and the festive note of the occasion, he confidently predicted the road would, in time, reach

The City Council of Fort Madison, Iowa passed an ordinance in 1886 giving the Chicago, Santa Fe and California Railroad the right to build in Iowa. The 1887 photo *at right* shows Santa Fe raised roadway construction being done on Fort Madison's Mississippi shore.

☞ NOW IS THE TIME TO BUY. ☜

"THE BEST THING IN THE WEST."

LEAVE YOUR STUMPS AND GRUBS

FOR A FARM ALREADY CLEARED.

PRODUCTS WILL PAY FOR LAND AND IMPROVEMENTS.

A HEALTHY CLIMATE, RICH SOIL AND PURE WATER.

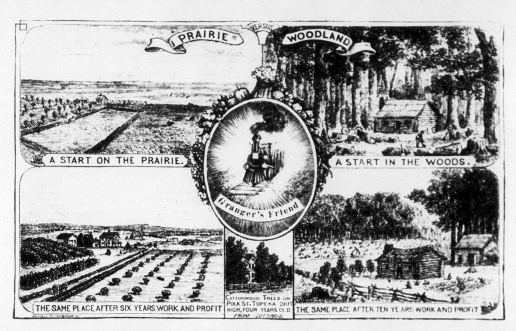

PRAIRIE VERSUS WOODLAND

A START ON THE PRAIRIE.

Granger's Friend

A START IN THE WOODS.

THE SAME PLACE AFTER SIX YEARS WORK AND PROFIT

COTTONWOOD TREES ON POLK ST. TOPEKA 26 FT HIGH, FOUR YEARS OLD FROM CUTTINGS.

THE SAME PLACE AFTER TEN YEARS WORK AND PROFIT

THE RICH VALLEY

LAND$

OF THE

Atchison, Topeka and Santa Fe R. R. Co.

SITUATED ON THE BEAUTIFUL

COTTONWOOD AND ARKANSAS RIVERS.

IN SOUTH-WESTERN KANSAS.

3,000,000 ACRES

FOR SALE ON ELEVEN YEARS' CREDIT.

Send for a large circular, giving full information about PRICES OF LAND, TERMS OF SALE, DISCOUNTS FOR IMPROVEMENTS, Exploring Tickets, and Rebate of Fares to Land Buyers. Address,

A. S. JOHNSON, Acting Land Commissioner,
Topeka, Kansas.

PLENTY OF RICH GOVERNMENT LANDS FOR HOMESTEADS.

the Pacific Coast and as an afterthought he added the Gulf of Mexico. Those present who did not laugh outright smiled tolerantly at what they felt were the ravings of a 'lunatic.'

Settling Kansas

The new railroad headed neither for Atchison nor Santa Fe but east toward the nearby Kaw River. Before the road could be built, it had to bridge the river and establish a connection with the Kansas Pacific. Once this task had been accomplished, the road built south, nearly to Burlingame and its excellent coal deposits—which furnished both traffic and fuel for the infant line.

Santa Fe's first train—the *Wakarusa Picnic Special*—rolled out of Topeka on 26 April 1869, carrying dignitaries and company officials. Tracks had been laid for only seven miles to Pauline and the remaining five miles to Wakarusa were covered by buggies and wagons.

The Santa Fe was operating 28 miles of track by 1869. By 1871, the construction gangs had reached Dodge City, the legendary and infamous town where 'disagreements' were settled with guns as often as not. Like other cattle towns along the Kansas frontier, Dodge City was important to the Santa Fe as a railhead for the large herds of longhorn cattle driven up from Texas on the 'Old Chisolm Trail.'

The 4-4-0 locomotive *Thomas Sherlock* (below) was built at the Santa Fe's Taunton shops in 1870. *At left:* Promotionals like this lured farmers westward, and thus built business for the Santa Fe.

Until the early 1870s, the Kansas Pacific Railroad had a virtual monopoly on the cattle trade to Chicago. But now the expanding Santa Fe Railway wanted to cross Kansas south of Abilene, taking some of the Kansas Pacific's business with it.

The cattle towns served another function in the West of the 1870s—they were the major points for the shipping of buffalo hides. The giant herds of buffalo that wandered the great plains were especially plentiful in Kansas, but unfortunately the coming of the railroads heralded their doom. Buffalo robes and coats were the height of fashion in Europe and the eastern United States.

Trade in buffalo hides was so lucrative that professional hunters slaughtered the animals by the millions. Even passengers and crews on the Santa Fe got into the act, shooting buffalo from passenger cars and locomotives just for sport. Tourists paid for exotic buffalo-hunting excursions, and were responsible for killing thousands of the beasts.

The Santa Fe track gangs worked their way westward, reaching the Colorado border in 1872, a full year ahead of the deadline set by Congress. (It was also just three years after the completion of the important transcontinental railroad.)

Track gangs on the Santa Fe—and other Western railways—were composed of Civil War veterans, mostly Irish, and a few local farm boys who drove horses and mule teams. Miserable working conditions prevailed. Summers were hot and the men worked long days under a pound-

ing sun. Winters brought freezing rain and snow. The construction camps in which the men lived consisted of sheds built of scrap lumber. Meals were limited to beans, saltpork, bread, sorghum and occasional buffalo meat.

Professional gamblers and prostitutes followed the camps in which in turn followed the railhead as it headed west. Dancehalls and saloons spelled trouble for the railworkers, who did not mix well with the frontier cattle drivers—or cowboys. They often argued and fought. Sometimes such altercations led to injury and death.

As the tracks moved ever-westward, the Santa Fe realized that Kansas was not populated heavily enough to generate sufficient business. If no one was farming the land, and there were no towns to serve farmers' needs, there could also be no freight or passenger business. So the Santa Fe set about settling the region.

The railroad opened a land department, which published booklets and pamphlets to lure new settlers. Agents were appointed in the new towns, the East and Europe to push the sale of lands. Tons of literature was distributed. Land-seekers were given special rates, usually half-fare, and the price of the ticket could be applied to the purchase price of the land.

The Santa Fe Railway's immigration program, however, got off to a shaky start. In the 1870s, Kansas suffered several grasshopper plagues and droughts. The Santa Fe

seemed near disaster when the grasshoppers came to Kansas. Crops were devoured and starving settlers were returning to the East in 1874. With the coming of the droughts, crops withered and thousands of farm animals died. As people fled Kansas for parts of the country with less grasshoppers and more water, the Santa Fe was plunged into the red. They made it through, however, but not without some help from an unusual group of immigrants.

It was in 1894 that the great influx of Mennonites from Russia began. They arrived in Topeka amid jeers at their strange ways and dress. The jeers soon became cheers when it was discovered they were well-financed. Undaunted by blizzards, droughts or grasshoppers, they purchased the equipment of the settlers returning to the East and set about preparing their lands and building houses. Their most important contribution was popularizing growing and milling the hard red Turkish wheat they had brought from Russia. This meant millions of dollars to the grain country and to the Santa Fe over the years.

The Santa Fe cut its rates, land prices and hauled building material free for a year. It even chartered liners to bring the settlers from Europe, and they came—from Germany, Sweden, Russia and Italy. The cattle towns and ranchers did not appreciate the fences strung by these hard-working farmers but the fences stayed and the farmers were tremendously successful with the land.

Cyrus Holliday's vision proved true, as the late 19th century photo *on these pages* shows a Santa Fe 'wharf railroad' operation on the West Coast. Just as the sailing ships in the background were—even as of this vintage photo—on their way to obsolescence, so too steam locomotives—such as the trusty little 0–6–0 yard switcher shown here—would eventually be outmoded by diesel power.

During the drought years, the Santa Fe hauled enormous tonnages free to save its settlers. It hauled thousands of bushels of seed grain free to farmers. The railroad's efforts to save its settlers paid off; colonies of successful farmers were established.

The Santa Fe earned its reputation as a well-run, sensibly managed railroad during this troubled period. A railroad magazine of the time even called it 'one of the best roads west of the Mississippi.'

Eventually, Mother Nature sorted herself out again. The grasshopper plague subsided and the rains returned. The Santa Fe recovered financially, and was now free to continue its expansion through the golden West.

Construction Into Colorado

There was ample inducement for extending the line westward into Colorado. Large coal deposits around Canon City and Trinidad promised large eastbound tonnage. Colorado timber would provide settlers in Kansas with direly-needed lumber. The mining industry with its proven reserves of precious metals would develop rapidly with improved transportation. This held forth the lure of heavy traffic in eastbound ores and, equally important, would create an increasing demand for mining machinery and manufactured goods from cities east of the Missouri River.

Santa Fe's gateway to the interior of Colorado was the city of Pueblo, where a connection would be made with an existing road to Denver. A line through Trinidad would approach the New Mexico boundary where much of the overland wagon traffic could be attracted to the railroad. Colorado offered virtually limitless traffic and it was decided to build to Pueblo, 138 miles west of Granada.

The first 50 miles to Las Animas were completed and ready for operation on 13 September 1875. On 1 March 1876 the line to Pueblo was placed in regular service.

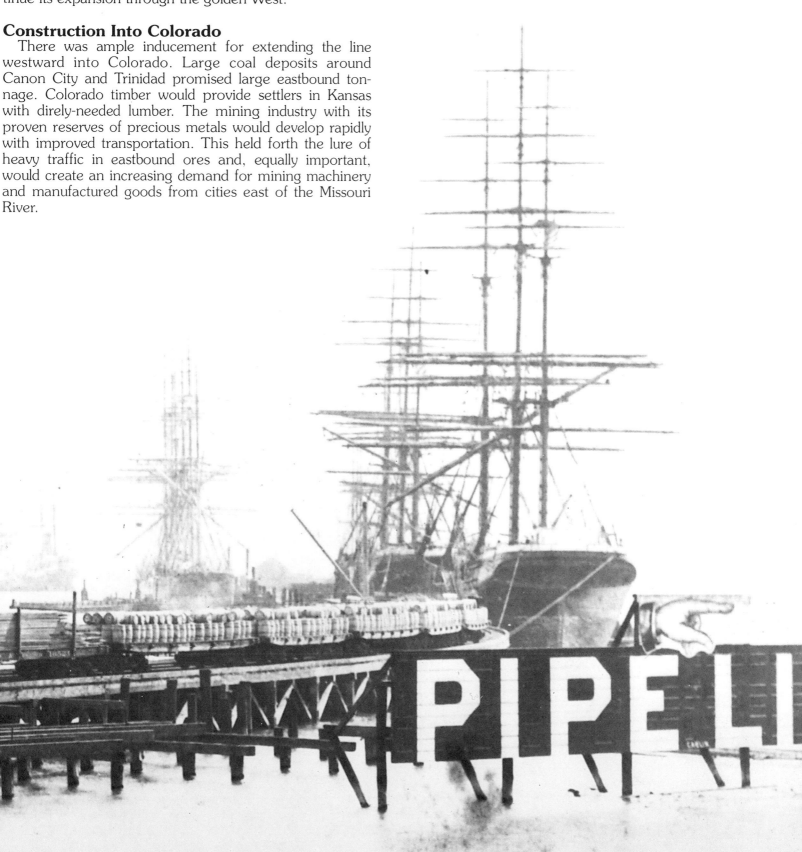

Wars in the Canyons of Colorado

by Thomas York

The ATSF reached the Kansas-Colorado border in 1872, one year ahead of the 10-year deadline set by Congress to claim title to the land grants. Continued progress also set the stage for a showdown with another competitor, the Denver & Rio Grande (D&RG) Railroad, which had expansion plans of its own in Colorado.

William Jackson Palmer, who had been a Union cavalry general in the Civil War, organized the Denver & Rio Grande in 1870 to build southward from Denver to El Paso and then on to Mexico City. Palmer wanted to push his railroad into New Mexico as much as the ATSF wanted to reach Pueblo and Canyon City, already served by the D&RG.

By this time, Boston financiers Thomas and Joseph Nickerson had wrested control of the ATSF from Holliday (although he stayed on as secretary of the board of directors). These two brothers recognized the need to expand the business of the railroad beyond carrying cattle and buffalo hides. They wanted to generate revenue from the various types of mining opportunities available in the Rocky Mountains of Colorado.

Palmer did not want to build a railroad competing against the Santa Fe, so he traveled east to persuade the new owners of the ATSF to cooperate in building one line. But his mission failed, setting up a confrontation for control of two important mountain passes—Raton Pass from Colorado into New Mexico and the Royal Gorge in southern Colorado.

The first clash came in early 1873. Legal rights to the 8000-foot Raton Pass, located 15 miles south of Trinidad, Colorado, were ambiguous. Both railroads claimed title, although Thomas Nickerson did not see the urgency of crossing the pass to get to Santa Fe.

Wagon traffic between Santa Fe and Colorado was not that heavy, and Nickerson did not believe that the line would support a rail service. But Holliday convinced Nickerson and others on the ATSF board of directors of the need to expand into New Mexico.

Nickerson sent survey crews south to where Palmer had already ordered surveys. Nickerson leased the rights to construct the new line over the pass to a new railroad, the Canyon City & San Juan. Yet the D&RG and the Santa Fe were not the only railroads battling for rights to New Mexico.

The Southern Pacific, under CP Huntington's shrewd leadership, was trying to stop the ATSF and the D&RG. Thomas Nickerson had ordered General Manager William Barstow Strong to approach the New Mexico state legislature to negotiate the required rights to build rail lines in the state. When Strong reached Santa Fe, however, he discovered that Southern Pacific representatives had beat him there.

The SP men had persuaded the lawmakers to require that the boards of the railroad operating in New Mexico be dominated by state residents. In addition, the law required the railroads to demonstrate that they possessed 10 percent of the building costs before starting work, which would make construction impossible for the Santa Fe.

Strong was not to be deterred, however. He stalked the halls of the state legislature, seeking a way to get around the law, and he found that the SP agents had left one loophole. They had neglected to get the New Mexico lawmakers to repeal the old law. Still in force therefore and superseding the new law, the old legislation allowed the Santa Fe to proceed without meeting the new requirements! Strong immediately created a new corporation—the New Mexico & Southern Pacific Railroad Com-

At right: **Through the yellowed celluloid of photographic time, a big Santa Fe 4-8-4 races along the trackage of another era. Long before even this, the Santa Fe was fighting for its rail routes.**

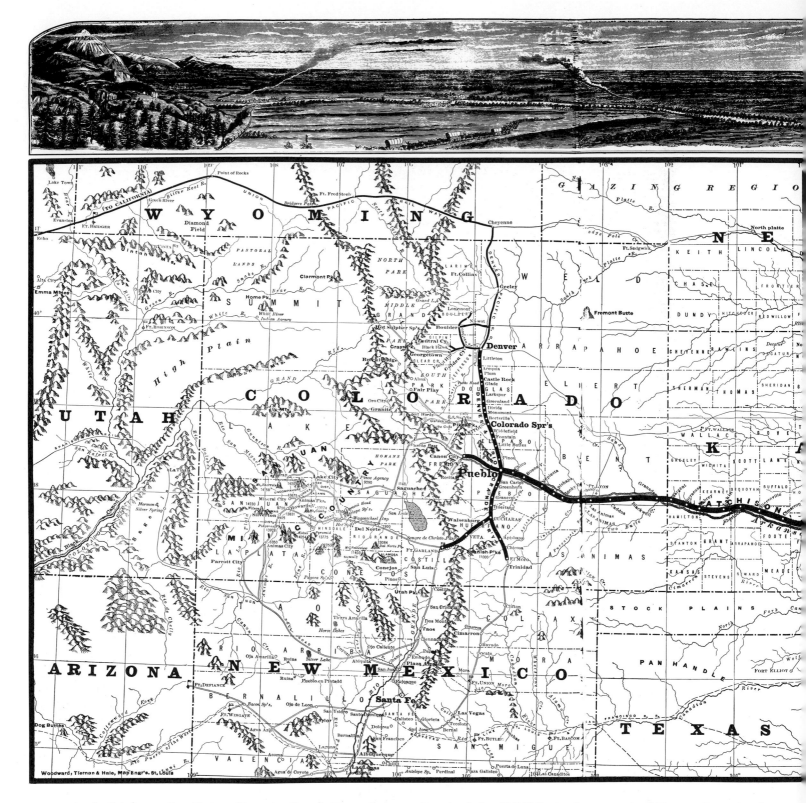

pany—to build from the Raton Pass to the Arizona border. He even convinced the lawmakers to exempt the new line from taxes for six years.

With business in Santa Fe completed, the stage was set for a construction battle with the D&RG for the Raton Pass. Strong returned to Kansas and instructed his crews to prepare to build a line across the Raton Pass—using force if necessary. He took a train to Trinidad where he recruited a small army of men and armed them with rifles and shovels. Palmer, on his side, had already recruited armed men to fight for control of the pass.

The opposing forces arrived at the mouth of Raton Pass on the same day in 1873. Men from the two railroads growled at each other, but the expected fight did not erupt. The Santa Fe, having arrived just minutes ahead of the D&RG, took control of Raton Pass, and its track crews went to work the next day.

On 7 December 1878, the first train traveled over Raton Pass by means of a switchback. The next year, crews bored a 2000-foot tunnel through the summit, reducing the maximum grade from 316 feet per mile to 185. The Santa Fe finally had reached New Mexico—after more than a decade.

The contest for Raton Pass was not the last time the two railroads would battle over Colorado real estate. Later, the ATSF and the Rio Grande fought for control of the Grand Canyon of the Arkansas (called the Royal Gorge), a narrow rift 3000 feet deep through granite Rockies west of Pueblo, leading to lucrative coal fields.

Once again, Strong ordered armed men into action and

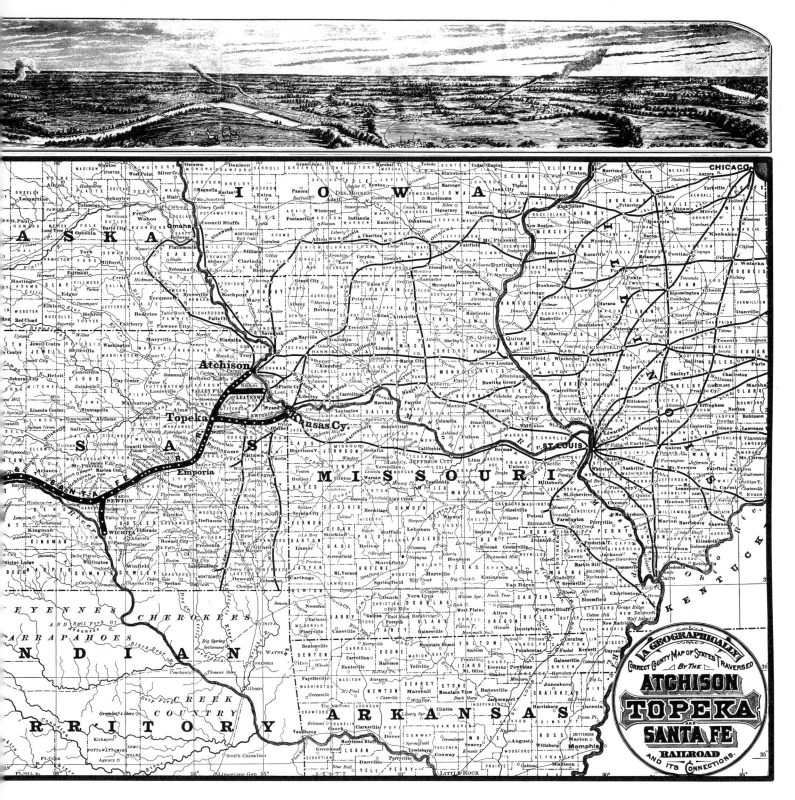

A GEOGRAPHICALLY CORRECT COUNTY MAP OF STATES TRAVERSED BY THE ATCHISON TOPEKA AND SANTA FE RAILROAD AND ITS CONNECTIONS.

sent them to the Royal Gorge to prevent D&RG crews from advancing. He also ordered one of his engineers, William R Morley, to round up reinforcements from Canyon City. Morley, however, could not travel on D&RG trains, so he had to ride 63 miles on horseback to get help. Morley's horse died from exhaustion but he saved the day for Santa Fe.

Meanwhile, Palmer and 200 armed men boarded a train and traveled to the mouth of the gorge, prepared to do battle. Morley led his own armed group back to the mouth of the canyon to confront Palmer and told the band of men recruited by the Denver & Rio Grande that he would use all necessary force to stop them.

'We got here first, and we're building the Canyon City & San Juan Railroad through to the Arkansas,' he

shouted. 'Anyone interfering with this work is liable to stop a bullet between the eyes.' They decided not to fight, allowing the Santa Fe to take control of the pass.

Thwarted, Palmer went to court to stop the Santa Fe from encroaching further into his domain, but his legal fight was unsuccessful. The court gave the Santa Fe a lockhold lease on the D&RG, and the ATSF assumed operational control of the competing line.

Palmer returned to the courts, claiming that the Santa Fe was violating its lease agreement by raising the rates on the Rio Grande line prohibitively high, thus diverting traffic to the Santa Fe and attempting to bankrupt the D&RG. When the Colorado Supreme Court returned control of the embattled line to Palmer in June 1879, he sent armed detachments to the Royal Gorge Canyon to block the Santa Fe from operating there. The men arrived and ordered Santa Fe to stop work 'by authority of the Supreme Court and the 50 rifles you see here.'

While heavily armed sheriff's deputies distributed the court order to Santa Fe employees operating the D&RG trains and depots, Rio Grande employees commandeered a Santa Fe train, retaking stations from El Moro to Pueblo, and open warfare soon erupted between employees from the two lines. Santa Fe crews operating trains on the Rio Grande tracks were attacked and beaten and their families were threatened.

The showdown came at Pueblo, where Rio Grande crews were met by Bat Masterson, the famous Dodge City marshal. Masterson, who boasted a long list of legally justified killings, had been imported to protect the Santa Fe's property. He had with him a gang of armed men to keep the property safe from Rio Grande employees.

As the Rio Grande train approached, loaded with armed men, Masterson ordered his gang to surround the roundhouse where the train would stop at Pueblo, and

told them to prepare to shoot. But no shots were fired. When the Rio Grande boys saw Masterson and his men with their revolvers, carbines and shotguns drawn, the threat was more than enough to stop a fight.

Under a white flag of truce, leaders from the two armed camps discussed the issue. The Rio Grande forces decided to buy off Masterson, thus retaking the Pueblo roundhouse without violence. Masterson and his men, being in this case complete mercenaries, readily complied. Their pockets now jingling with more money, the contented Masterson and his merry men lay down their arms and left peaceably under the protection of law officers.

The war was not yet over. The dispatcher's office remained in the hands of Santa Fe men, who were not about to give ground. When Rio Grande men assaulted the office with a barrage of bullets, two men were killed and two were injured.

Finally the two sides, tired of the ensuing guerrilla warfare, came to a conference table in Boston in February 1880. Santa Fe voluntarily gave up its lease with Rio Grande and the rights to the Royal Gorge Canyon. In essence, the Santa Fe was allowed to continue its transcontinental conquest while the Denver & Rio Grande was allowed to expand locally in Colorado.

The feisty Denver & Rio Grande intended that only its own stock, such as the 2–6–0 Mogul class loco shown below**, should roll in Colorado. The deadly but easily swayed Bat Masterson** (opposite) **was, very briefly, a deciding factor in the Santa Fe-D&RG wars.**

Yet it was a hollow victory for Palmer. The D&RG remained a troubled line for years to come, undergoing three bankruptcies in the ensuing years.

Las Vegas was reached in July, 1879. The main line had pushed through Glorietta Pass and dropped down to Lamy in the Rio Grande Valley. By this time the ultimate destination was the Pacific Coast and the main line was to follow the Rio Grande to Albuquerque.

It was a grave disappointment to learn that the road's main line could not be routed through the long-sought city of Santa Fe, but the surveys indicated there was no practical way to build west out of town. The citizenry of Santa Fe was determined to have rail service and approved a bond issue to aid in constructing a branch line from Lamy. Thus, the first Santa Fe train to the namesake city arrived 16 February 1880. Holliday's dream had been realized. Perhaps the other early objectives—the Pacific, the Gulf of Mexico and Chicago—were not ridiculous after all.

Albuquerque was reached 15 April 1880 and six months later tracks were laid as far south as San Marcial without any sign of stopping. A connection at Deming, with another road building east from California, on 8 March 1881, gave the nation its second transcontinental line.

Straight and Steady

Rails from East to West

Expansion of the Santa Fe both east and west was begun in 1875. Kansas City had become the terminus of practically all the important railroads in the area and was rapidly emerging as the greatest cattle and grain market of the Southwest. In view of the fact that grain and cattle comprised the bulk of Santa Fe's eastbound traffic, and Kansas City lay a mere 67 miles east of Topeka, it became essential to secure directly served terminal facilities at Kansas City.

Reaching this growing metropolis would provide ready markets for grain and livestock thereby stimulating growth of this eastbound traffic. Too, Santa Fe stood to gain considerable westbound traffic, both freight and passenger. Access to this potential traffic was gained on 1 October 1875, when the company leased the Kansas City, Topeka and Western, an existing road between Kansas City and Topeka.

During this period of growth, the Atchison, Topeka and Santa Fe decided to keep building westward from New Mexico to California. New Mexico did not have a large farming population that the railroad could serve, and since farmers were the main source of railroad business and revenue, the best move seemed to be expansion into bountiful California.

Santa Fe officials felt all of the freight traffic to Arizona and much destined for Southern California would naturally move over the new and shorter transcontinental route. The connecting line, which was already handling this traffic from San Francisco, saw no reason to share its revenues with this invader from the East. They felt it would be better to have the goods move to San Francisco over the Central Pacific-Union Pacific route and then south and east on their road.

The Santa Fe bought a half interest in a charter owned by the St Louis & San Francisco Railway, also known as the 'Frisco.' This would permit them to move into California. No one in the company knew then that Jay Gould and C P Huntington owned controlling interest in the Frisco line. These two investors had no intention of letting the Santa Fe cross the Colorado river into California, thus enabling it to compete with the Southern Pacific and the Texas & Pacific. To this end, they flatly refused to establish rates which would enable goods to move over the new route. The Santa Fe was at the mercy of its competition.

Another Santa Fe attempt to reach the ports of San Francisco and San Diego met the same fate. In a joint venture, the Santa Fe and a cooperative midwestern railroad purchased the struggling Atlantic & Pacific railroad. Under the name and charter of the Atlantic & Pacific, a new line was built west from Albuquerque through Arizona. Recognizing the threat posed by this line and still desirous of maintaining their stranglehold, the competition gained control of the cooperating midwestern road. No action could be taken without consent of both roads which meant that the tracks of the Atlantic and Pacific were stopped at Needles, California. The competition did build a line north from Mojave to Needles, California, the end of Atlantic & Pacific construction, ostensibly giving Santa Fe access to the Pacific Coast.

Once again the situation proved intolerable and Santa Fe made arrangements for obtaining or building parallel or shorter routes. Either alternative would have rendered the newly-built Mojave to Needles line worthless and it was sold to the Atlantic & Pacific at cost in 1884. At the same time, an agreement providing for joint trackage to San Francisco was negotiated. Having finally reached the major Coast ports and no longer dependent on the good will of its competitor, Santa Fe expanded its California trackage through mergers and purchases of smaller lines.

Eventually, the Santa Fe acquired the Chicago, Cincinnati and St Louis Railway, which included track between Chicago and the Mississippi. To this line, it added trackage across the river, connecting with its own line in Kansas.

This trackage, along with the Frisco acquisition, gave the Santa Fe more than 7000 miles of track, with operations stretching from Chicago to the West Coast to the Gulf of Mexico.

From the turning of the first spade of Kansas earth on 30 October 1868, the little railroad had within a span of 20 years become one of the greatest systems in the world—a railroad that extended from the shores of Lake Michigan to the Pacific Coast, and the Gulf of Mexico. The dream of Cyrus K Holliday had been fulfilled.

After his success in the Colorado railroad wars, Strong had become president of the company. Under his leader-

At right: **Bell clanging loudly, this long Santa Fe passenger train nears a grade crossing. The poles and wires on either side of the track, like the train itself, were emblems of westward expansion.**

CYRUS K. HOLLIDAY
1826–1900
PIONEER AND BUILDER
FOUNDER AND MAYOR OF TOPEKA.
INFLUENCED THE SELECTION OF THIS CITY
AS THE CAPITAL OF KANSAS.
ORGANIZED THE ATCHISON, TOPEKA AND
SANTA FE RAILROAD COMPANY. OBTAINED
THE ORIGINAL CHARTER IN THE YEAR 1859.
PROMOTED THE EARLY DEVELOPMENT OF
KANSAS AND THE ENTIRE SOUTHWEST.

At left: **A vintage Santa Fe 4–4–0 and passenger train on Canyon Diablo bridge.** *Above:* **Topeka's Cyrus Holliday commemorative plaque.** *Overleaf:* **Wells Fargo versus the Santa Fe in a spontaneous race.**

ship, expansion and innovation continued. Strong spent money on improving and adding trackage and rolling stock. He ordered new, heavier steel tracks for the main rail lines, replacing old ties with treated ones, and increased equipment from 5530 units in 1880 to 32,293 units in 1895. He also brought larger, more powerful locomotives to the Santa Fe. Like other railroads, it had used 4–4–0s, but in the 1880s it began to use 2–6–0s and 4–6–0s from the Baldwin Locomotive Works. These were needed to pull the trains of ever-increasing length and load.

This impressive expansion did not protect the Santa Fe from the economic pressures which forced many railroads into bankruptcy in the late 1880 and 1890s. Santa Fe rates, revenues and earnings slid down as interest payments on the company debt climbed. The Atchison, Topeka & Santa Fe fell into receivership.

Edward Ripley took over as president in 1896 and saved the line. Under his guidance, total trackage grew to more than 11,000 miles and the foundation was laid for new financial and administrative health of the company, which continues today.

Working on various railroads before coming to the Santa Fe, Ripley earned a reputation for integrity, honesty and leadership. He is credited with setting the standards that made the Santa Fe one of the most successful railroads in America.

Above: **This Santa Fe 0–4–0 switcher paused by the rolling waters of San Diego Harbor sometime in the 1880s. Its crew apparently was taking a lunch break in the fresh ocean air—a luxury the fellows who manned the 4–4–0** *on the facing page* **couldn't share in the dusty environs of the Santa Fe's El Paso, Texas station, where this photo was taken.**

The Santa Fe began to win the trust of the people it served and proved itself a force to be reckoned with, when Ripley brought the railroad to San Francisco at the request of farmers and growers. The move was planned to counter Southern Pacific's de facto monopoly on freight trains and traffic in Northern California. The Southern Pacific was charging exorbitant local rates to move goods and products from the Central Valley to San Francisco. Rates were even higher for transcontinental routes. San Francisco shippers, fed up with the practice, organized the San Francisco Traffic Association to fight it and asked Ripley and the Santa Fe for help. They wanted to build an independent railroad from Stockton through the San Joaquin Valley to San Francisco.

Claus Spreckles, a California sugar tycoon, took the lead in the project, contributing enough money to convince other investors to participate. A state charter was introduced in Sacramento for the San Francisco and San Joaquin Valley Railroad, which became known as 'The People's Railroad.' The Santa Fe bought controlling interest in the little railroad and continues to operate on the track today.

By the time the battle for access to the Pacific subsided in 1884, the Santa Fe's network of branch lines throughout Kansas had been considerably strengthened and expanded.

That same year, with eyes on the Gulf of Mexico, the Santa Fe received Congressional authority to build south from Arkansas City, Kansas, through Indian Territory. The Gulf, Colorado and Santa Fe, a Galveston based road, had also obtained rights to build north across the Territory. The GC&SF ran into financial difficulties and a contract for its sale to Santa Fe was negotiated with the provision that it would build north from Fort Worth, Texas, and connect with the line Santa Fe was building from Arkansas City. The rails were bolted together at Purcell on 26 April 1887—with the discovery of tremendous oil reserves and the great land rushes (to settle what is now Oklahoma) still in the future.

Congressional permission to build across the Territory south also provided for construction of a railroad from Kiowa, Kansas, through Waynoka to the south and west. On 12 September 1887, rails were laid across the Texas state line and the road continued to Panhandle City and later Amarillo. This road eventually became part of the Santa Fe's present mainline through the Texas Panhandle.

It was evident by 1883 that the Santa Fe should build to Chicago, which was even then well on its way to becoming

the 'railroad center of the world.' The engineer for the project drew a straight line between Kansas City and Chicago as the desired route. Locators were warned not to plan any curve they could not account for. It was eventually decided to purchase and rebuild the Chicago and St Louis and use about 100 miles of it as the new line.

After a highly secretive location survey and right-of-way acquisition campaign, which began in 1885 and lasted until December, 1886, the Santa Fe established construction offices in Kansas City and Chicago and started building between those points in March, 1887. Since the surveyed line intersected 13 other roads, the operation was greatly simplified. Construction of this segment still stands as an outstanding achievement in railroading. In nine months, some 350 miles of new line were built, about 100 miles of old line were completely rebuilt, and five large bridges were erected across major rivers.

Terminal facilities in Chicago were acquired by purchase or lease of various short lines which, when pieced together, provided an excellent route to the leased Dearborn Station. This 'airline' even today gives the Santa Fe the shortest and fastest route between the two major cities. In January, 1888, train service was begun and regular operations commenced on May 1.

Conception and realization of Holliday's dream was accomplished largely through the leadership, energy and devotion of CK Holliday and WB Strong and Edward

Ripley. Magnificent though it was, the dream served only as the base for the growth of the Santa Fe—the beginning, as it were. The Santa Fe today, with its subsidiary operations and a modern railroad plant second to none, was built step by step under the guidance of many men—men of great vision.

Each of these men has made his contribution and left his imprint etched on the pages of the Santa Fe's history. Its second century of progress will undoubtedly see other names added to the list as having made equally great contributions.

Steam Power

Few inventions have played so important a part in the growth and progress of our nation as the steam locomotive.

The horsepower of the covered wagon and stage coach became steam power as the railroads stretched west. For over 150 years the steam locomotive did an important job for our nation's railroads, but when the modern diesel locomotive appeared on the scene, it marked the beginning of the end of an era.

The Santa Fe Railway owned more than 3000 steam locomotives throughout its history, and they participated in many historical events. There is the epic of Nelly Bly, who made part of her trip 'Around the World in 80 Days' behind a Santa Fe steamer from San Francisco to

Chicago. And Death Valley Scotty who, in 1905, plunked down $5500 in cash for a private train that would take him from Los Angeles to Chicago 'faster than any cow-puncher ever rode before'—setting a record that stood until broken by the diesel.

Santa Fe became completely dieselized in 1954, although a power shortage during the heavy wheat harvest of 1955 made it necessary to call on several of the retired veteran steam locos for a helping hand for a few months. But even before then the gallant steamers were assuming a new role, as cities along the Santa Fe right-of-way began to· seek a locomotive for display in their community. The first went to Travel Town in Los Angeles' Griffith Park, on 22 May 1953, and was followed by 45 others. The last one given away went to the Museum of Transport at St Louis, Mo, in November, 1962.

Santa Fe has retained for posterity four steam locomotives. They are the *Cyrus K Holliday,* a replica of the road's first engine; the *Little Buttercup,* another early-day locomotive used in pageants; the 1010, the last remaining engine from the Death Valley Scotty run; and the 2925, one of the most modern steam locomotives ever built.

A Classic Symbol

It was 33 years between the time the first shovel of dirt was turned for the building of the Santa Fe and the adoption of the railroad's trademark.

Simple in design, but distinctive in appearance, the Santa Fe's present trademark is well-known to the nation's shippers and travellers.

The present Santa Fe trademark was adopted in 1901, but its history began in 1888 when the original design, a rectangle with rounded corners resembling a cake of soap, and the legend 'Santa Fe Route' in the center, was adopted.

This first attempt was followed in 1895 by a 'lion and globe,' representing the king of beasts surmounting the globe, on the face of which was shown a map of the United States with 'Santa Fe Route' on the folds of a pennant as its base. At the time, Santa Fe was considered the 'big line' of the United States and was advertised as 'the greatest railroad in the world, with 9346 miles of track.' The lion was innocently placed on the top of the globe bearing the map of America, and drew considerable criticism. Some maintained that a foreign country, the Dominion of Canada, was being advertised and that the lion, standing on Canadian soil, represented the British lion.

In 1896 the 'cake of soap' form again became the trademark of the Santa Fe, but unlike the first emblem, was placed square with the form on which it was used.

Today there are numerous versions of why, where and how the present Santa Fe trademark had its origin.

James Marshall, author of *Santa Fe, The Railroad That Built an Empire,* relates that the present trademark

The history of the Santa Fe's motive power is shown *below*, left to right—from early steam to modern diesel. Even at this, the story continues, for advanced diesel road switchers with modular electronic components have replaced even the powerful engines shown here.

Evolution of the Santa Fe Logo

| 1888-1895 | 1895-1896 | 1896-1899 | 1899-1901 | 1901-Present |

was conceived in 1897 by JJ Byrne, a passenger traffic manager at Los Angeles, California. Paul Morton, Santa Fe vice president in charge of traffic, took exception to the trademark, then current, which bore the words, 'Santa Fe Route.' He maintained that it was inconsistent to use 'Santa Fe,' which is of Spanish origin and means 'Holy Faith' with 'route' which is obviously French. Morton called in his traffic representatives, GT Nicholson, WJ Black and JJ Byrne, and asked for ideas. During the conference, so the story goes, Byrne, a Westerner, removed a silver dollar from his pocket and penciled a line around

it. Next he squared the circle on the outside, drew a cross within the circle and wrote 'Santa Fe' on the cross arm. Byrne said the idea of the cross came from 'Holy Faith.'

According to another legend, in 1901 a couple of officials were discussing the design for a trademark, when one of them traced a circle with a silver dollar to symbolize wheels of transportation. Inside he placed a cross to which he assigned a triple meaning: First, it symbolized the four points of the compass; second, it was the cross carried by the Franciscan padres during the explorations of the Spanish conquistadores in the Southwest; third, it

was the pagan sign of the sun used by the Indians centuries before white men set foot in the colorful lands of the Santa Fe.

In a story which appeared in the November 1908 Santa Fe Magazine and was reprinted again in January 1929, it is stated that the trademark was designed in February 1901 on train Number Two going into Chicago. Industrial Commissioner Davis and JJ Byrne were discussing trademarks—Santa Fe's in particular. In a rough way the emblem as it now appears was then devised, a silver dollar being used to draw the circle surrounding the cross. This trademark was adopted the same year.

Freeman H Habbard, author of *Railroad Avenue,* has another version of the birth of the emblem. On company business aboard a Pullman, some Santa Fe executives were experimenting with emblems. One design was put on a poker chip. It was the cross and circle that the New Mexican Indians had used to symbolize the Christian faith. The cross within a circle stood for the sun god that the Indians worshipped.

Still another meaning of the Santa Fe trademark is that along with the three basic symbols of design—circle, cross and square—it comprises the three basic ideals of doing business: soundness, good faith and four-square integrity.

To the Indians of the Southwest, the cross symbolizes the four directions of the compass and the crossing of roads. The circle indicates the world and symbolizes the wheel, a fundamental of transportation. The cross, of course, has an added religious significance and is suggestive of the fact that in Spanish 'Santa Fe' means 'Holy Faith.'

The traditional story is that Byrne devised the present design. Being a student of the Southwest, he knew that the cross was symbolical of not only the pagan Indians, but also the Spanish Christians who explored and developed that territory. With this thought in mind he took a silver dollar and drew a circle to represent transportation, placed a cross within it and wrote the words, 'Santa Fe' on the transverse bar. Possibly to give his creation three of the basic designs, he set the cross and circle within a square.

Officially, the railroad is The Atchison, Topeka & Santa Fe Railway Company, so the trademark is a concession to passengers, freight men, officials and railroad buffs who have always called it the Santa Fe. Atchison and Topeka were outposts on the Kansas frontier when Cyrus Holliday first had his dream of building a railroad—westward across the Rockies and the desert, via Santa Fe to the Pacific.

The trademark appears as a cross within a circle, and as a cross within a circle within a square. Both are official. Today, 100 years after the first Santa Fe emblem, it may well have a different meaning to each individual. To the shipper it means service and dependability with the most modern facilities in rail transportation. To the traveler it means a most enjoyable and luxurious trip. To the rail fan, the emblem brings forth the most fascinating hobby in the world. To its employes, the Santa Fe trademark really symbolizes the soundness, good faith and four-square integrity already mentioned.

At right: This turn-of-the-century photo depicts the Santa Fe's Richmond, California roundhouse as its 'table' is being turned to receive the engine at photo right. *Overleaf:* A Santa Fe 10-wheeler hauls the first of the famed *California Limiteds* into Los Angeles.

The Fred Harvey Story

Frederick Henry Harvey has often been credited with civilizing the West. Certainly, he brought gastronomic delights and hospitality beyond many cattlemen's wildest dreams to a business sorely in need of them.

Before Harvey made his mark, food along the rails was notorious. Dining cars had not yet made their appearance, so meals were served at railroad depots. Trains had to stop at mealtimes, usually for only 10 minutes. Passengers paid about 50 cents in advance for a lunch or supper of rancid bacon, canned beans, eggs, bitter coffee and 'sinkers'—heavy biscuits.

To top it all off, these road houses were often in league with the train crews. Almost as soon as the customers were served, the train whistle blew, the conductor called 'All aboard!' and the passenger had to make a run for the train, leaving most of the meal uneaten. The beanery served what was left to the next victim, and paid off the train crew at a dime a passenger.

Enter Fred Harvey, a low-key, gentlemanly Englishman with exquisite taste and appreciation for good food and pleasant surroundings. Under his guidance, the Santa Fe gained a reputation for fine dining and hospitality unsurpassed by any American railroad before or since.

Harvey was born in London in 1835, the son of a Scottish-English couple. At the age of 15, about the same time Cyrus Holliday was studying to become a Pennsylvania lawyer, Harvey left England with $10 and a ticket to New York in his pocket. A few days after arriving, he got a job as a 'pot whalloper' at the Smith & McNeill restaurant and bar at 229 Washington St.

Somehow, he managed to save a few dollars from his meager salary, and once again used his savings for passage, this time to New Orleans. After a bout with yellow fever, he got another restaurant job, then used the savings from it to buy a ticket to St Louis.

By now it was 1853, and St Louis—the 'Gateway to the West'—was a bustling, vibrant city of 150,000. Waterfront warehouses, smoking factories and river paddle wheelers provided the backdrop for the realization of young Fred Harvey's dream—to open his own restaurant. By 1859, he had found a partner and opened a successful eating place. In 1860, he married 18-year-old Barbara Sarah Mattas ('Sally'), a beautiful Bohemian girl born in Prague.

Fred Harvey (at right), 'the man who civilized the West,' saw to it that the Santa Fe's passengers got first-rate meals. *Above:* Two good-natured Harvey girls at the Hutchinson, Kansas Harvey House in 1910.

But this happy and prosperous time was not to last. With the outbreak of the Civil War in 1861, Harvey's business partner, who, unlike Harvey, sympathized with the South, absconded with all the restaurant funds, leaving the young entrepreneur with no business and no money.

Harvey then went to work for the Mississippi River Packet Line owned by Captain Rufus Ford, which ran to St Joseph. In 1862, Harvey was hired as a distributing clerk in the St Joseph mailroom, then as a postal worker on the mail cars on the Hannibal & St Joseph Railroad— a pioneering Western railroad known more widely as the 'Horrible and Slow Jolting.' This was Harvey's introduc-

tion to the deplorable state of railroad food and accommodations, and the beginning of his long association with the rails.

By 1865, Harvey had risen in the railroad business to become the general western agent for the North Missouri Railroad, and was transferred to Leavenworth, where he eventually purchased a home. The house is still a Leavenworth showplace, and is now on the National Register of Historic Places. Built by AA Higginbotham in 1875 and sold to Harvey for $24,856, the three-story building is made of sawn and hand-carved limestone; lacy detailing adorns the roof and the front entrance.

With his new-found prosperity, Harvey got into the restaurant business again. He and a partner, Jeff Rice, opened two eating establishments, one each in the Kansas towns of Hugo and Wallace. After a few months, the two men parted company, dividing up the profits. Harvey then went to the Burlington Railroad with an idea to provide quality food and service to travelers through cooperation between the railroad and himself. The Burlington wasn't interested.

Harvey approached Charles Morse, superintendent of the Santa Fe, whom he had known as a co-worker during a brief stint at the Burlington. Morse also appreciated fine dining, and thought that Harvey's ideas had possibilities. They persuaded WS Strong, Santa Fe's general manager at the time, to give it a try. Thus it was that the first Harvey House opened—in Topeka, Kansas.

Harvey purchased a small restaurant in the old Topeka depot and office building. He closed it down for two days, scrubbed it thoroughly, got new, high-quality tablecloths and napkins, polished the silver and stocked up on better food. The Santa Fe provided the space and some

materials and supplies on a handshake deal, which, for a very long time, was the only kind of deal Harvey made with the Santa Fe. He believed that when gentlemen did business, no other guarantee was needed.

Within a few weeks the Topeka eating house was doing a capacity business. The Santa Fe agreed that Harvey's experiment had been a success. They expanded the operation in 1877 and bought a rundown hotel on the line at Florence. Harvey and his wife and sister picked out mattresses, cooking equipment and heavy walnut furniture. Harvey ordered Sheffield silver from England and fine table linens from Ireland. The glassware was first-rate. The chef was hired away from Chicago's famed Palmer House for $5000 a year, making him easily the wealthiest man in Florence.

Florence was awed. A tiny hamlet of about 100 people with no inherent importance except the fact that it was on a railway, it had never seen the like of this Harvey House. Farmers prospered. The Chicago chef paid top prices for prairie chickens, quail, fresh butter, fruits and vegetables.

Word of mouth made the Florence house food and accommodations famous. Soon travelers were flocking to the Santa Fe because it was the only railroad that provided passengers with decent meals. The success of the Harvey Houses was measured in this way—by the passengers they brought to the Santa Fe; they were not expected to make large profits in and of themselves. Frequently they did not, and even lost money.

One Harvey House, for instance, consistently lost $1000 per month. When a new manager was hired, he sliced this loss to $500 per month by serving smaller portions and lower-quality food. He proudly boasted his achievement, until word of it reached Fred Harvey's ears.

Above left: Typical Harvey Girls in Syracuse, Kansas. *Above:* The huge Harvey House in Dodge City. *Right:* A Santa Fe ad touting Harvey service. *Overleaf:* The thematically rustic interior of the Hotel El Tovar at the Grand Canyon. Note the spitoons near the table legs.

Harvey fired the manager (although he eventually cooled off and placed him at another House). The Harvey House, to Mr Harvey's pleasure, went back to serving good food and losing $1000 per month.

As one of Harvey's sons explained in a 1921 article:

'Of course the opportunity to increase immediate profits by letting down on service grew as the business established itself. After the Florence Hotel got under way, for example, and people were talking about it, and more business was coming its way than it could handle, there was the usual opportunity to cash in on the good reputation to shade down service and shade up prices.

'My father was very well aware of this opportunity of course, but he also saw in the situation a peculiar opportunity to build good will. People would be expecting him to let down a little in his care for their interests under all this prosperity. And he saw that if he did not let them down then, they would notice it and appreciate it all the more, they would feel all the more that they could rely on his service. And again he did not let them down.'

Temptations to let customers down abounded, but Harvey gave in to none of them. There was, for instance, the milk problem in Arizona. Getting the necessary supplies to the restaurants was difficult during the early days of expansion in the Southwest. In those days milk could not be brought into Arizona from the dairy country, because the distance was too great and it would have spoiled; it could not be bought in the state because there were not sufficient milk-producing herds.

Santa Fe de-Luxe
The only extra fare train to California: extra fast and extra fine

California Limited
Also exclusively for first-class travel
Fred Harvey dining car meals
On the way visit that world-wonder
Grand Canyon of Arizona

Santa Fe
All the way

For art booklets of both trains address W J Black Passenger Traffic Manager
A·T·Q·S·F Railway System 1064 Railway Exchange, Chicago

Harvey did not have to supply milk. If he had not, he would not have suffered by comparison with other Arizona eateries. None of them had it. Customers would have understood that fresh milk was unobtainable in the deserts of Arizona.

But Harvey established his own dairy farm there to supply his Arizona houses. And when he had trouble because the right kind of cows could not be bought there and did not do well when they were shipped in, he established his own nursery for the cattle.

Even during the Depression, no skimping was allowed in a Harvey establishment. During one inspection it was revealed that a manager had stretched his meat supply to provide 156 steaks. He received a stern reprimand from his supervisor and was told that he should have gotten only 141 steaks from his supply. Harvey insisted on keeping the quality of food and service high and the cost to customers low. Meals cost 50 cents at first, then stayed at 75 cents until 1918, when they went up to $1. At lunch counters, where the price was even lower, the quality was as high but there was less of a variety of food.

A typical 75 cent Harvey menu in 1888 offered diners a diversity including blue points on shell, English peas au gratin, filet of whitefish in madeira sauce, potatoes francaise, young capon with hollandaise sauce, roast sirloin of beef au jus, pork with applesauce, stuffed turkey with cranberry sauce, mashed potatoes, sweet potatoes, Elgin sugar corn, marrowfat peas, asparagus in cream sauce, salmi of duck, queen olives, baked veal pie, charlotte of peaches with cognac sauce, prairie chicken with currant jelly, sugar cured ham, pickled lamb's tongue, lobster salad, beets, celery and french slaw. Then there were the dessert offerings of various fruits, ice cream, cakes and specialties, such as cold custard à la chantilly and catawba wine jelly, and cheeses with water crackers and coffee. Customers were welcome to partake of all of these dishes, although in practice they usually limited their choices to a few of these appetizing dishes.

The surroundings the meals were served in were no less impressive. After things got rolling, most of the Harvey Houses, especially those in the Southwest, were designed by architect Mary Colter. Colter had a keen sense of the Indian and Spanish heritage of the region, and planned the buildings with this in mind. At her suggestion, Native American motifs were used on walls, menus and even specially created china. Thus, from the foundations of the hotels to the smallest detail on the table, Harvey Houses blended beautifully with the landscape and the mood of the Southwest.

Fare and dining rooms such as Harvey offered would alone have assured return customers and a solid reputation, among both the train travelers and the locals (with whom the houses were equally popular). But as if these things weren't enough, Harvey introduced the Harvey Girls, and went on to 'win the West' as no bandit or lawman could have done.

Harvey wanted standards of service as high as his standards of cuisine. He placed ads in eastern and midwestern newspapers: 'Wanted: Young women of good character, attractive and intelligent, 18 to 30.' Experience was not essential, but good character was; under the

At right: **Harvey Girls abound in this 1926 photo of the Hutchinson, Kansas Harvey House. Evident here is the sparkling politesse amid which such as these gentlemen took their ease and dined well.**

stern, watchful eye of a veteran Harvey matron, girls were in by 10 o'clock, slept in dormitories, and did their hair plainly but prettily (no fancy hairdos allowed)—always tied in back with a simple white ribbon. Their uniforms of black dress, black stockings and black shoes had to be neatly cleaned and pressed at all times. They dished up welcome and good cheer, as well as meals, to customers.

Poems were written about them:
    'Oh, the pretty Harvey Girl beside my chair
    A fairer maiden I shall never see
    She was winsome, she was neat, she was gloriously sweet,
    And she certainly was very good to me,'
wrote SE Kiser, who later wrote yet another, longer ode to Harvey Girls:

'THE HARVEY GIRL
    I have seen some splendid paintings in my day
    And I have looked at faultless statuary;
    I've seen the orchard trees abloom in May
    And watched their colors in the shadows vary;
    I have viewed the noblest shrines in Italy
    And gazed upon the richest mosques of Turkey,
    But the fairest of all sights, It seems to me,
    Was a Harvey girl I saw in Albuquerque.

O that pretty Harvey girl was good to see,
    Her presence and her manner made me glad;
    As she heaped things on my plate,
    I kept busy thanking Fate
    For her deftness and the appetite I had.

I have heard the wind blow softly through the trees,
    I have listened to the robin blithely singing;
    I have heard the mellow sounds float on the breeze,
    When far-off matin bells were slowly ringing;
    I have heard great Paderewski pound the keys,
    But the pretty Harvey girl, as I'm a sinner,
    Produced the blithest of all melodies
    As she clicked the plates while handing me my dinner.'

J C Davis of Devore, California had this to say:
    'Harvey Houses, don't you savvy; clean across the old Mojave,
    On the Santa Fe they've strung 'em like a string of Indian beads,
    We all couldn't eat without 'em but the slickest thing about 'em,
    Is the Harvey skirts that hustle up the feeds.'

Writer Elbert Hubbard, reviewing Santa Fe service for his publication 'The Fra' in 1909, wrote:

Uniform changes can be deduced by comparing the 1926 photo *above*—of Harvey Girls and their house mothers—and the 1910 photo *right*. Harvey Houses and Hotels were individually, thematically designed, as this photo of Hotel La Posada's lunchroom *(left)* indicates.

'At Fred Harvey's you are always expected. The girls are ever in their best bib and tucker, spotlessly gowned, manicured, combed, dental flossed—bright, healthy, intelligent girls—girls that are never fly, flip nor fresh, but who give you the attention that never obtrudes, but which is hearty and heartfelt.

'You note the immaculate linen, the shining silver, the dainty fruits and flowers, and your heart is full of admiration for Fred Harvey, great and good, shy and modest, industrious and persistent, restless and brave, who set the world such a pace in catering that the effete and dreamy East can only imitate it.

'I have it on reliable authority of Mendelssohn himself, Tourist Agent, that a Fred Harvey girl lasts on the Desert only about six months, when she forfeits her pay, marries a millionaire mine owner or ranchman, and they settle down and are happy ever afterward. The first boy is always and forever named FH.'

It is said that Fred Harvey furnished the West with good food and fine wives. Despite the generous salary—$17.50 per month, room, board and tips (and Harvey Girls were usually tipped, and tipped well)—many girls did marry soon after beginning their employment. They had to promise verbally when signing up not to marry for a year. Harvey, however, accepted philosophically the fact that girls 'of good character, attractive and intelligent' wouldn't last long on the prairies and in the desert without being snatched up. He would frequently stage parties for the

Above: The Harvey House at Santa Fe station in Amarillo, Texas, circa 1926. *Below:* Harvey Girls such as these often met their future husbands while serving them meals. *Above right:* The Fred Harvey lunch counter at Santa Fe's Barstow, California station, in 1900.

newlyweds. But he also congratulated any girl who got through her first six months without an engagement ring. Experience was that if a Harvey girl could hold out that long, she usually stayed unmarried for another three or four years.

For the most part, the girls, with their demure decorum and poise, married quite well, either becoming brides of Santa Fe engineers, conductors or station agents, or well-to-do Western ranchers and farmers. The grand total of Harvey Girls who became Western wives has been estimated at 5000. There is also a legend, far from proven, that more than 4000 babies were christened 'Fred' or 'Harvey'—or both—after these marriages.

The Girls even inspired the movie *The Harvey Girls,* which starred Judy Garland. It is this film that is the source of the famous song extolling the virtues of the 'Atchison, Topeka and the Santa Fe.'

Another point in Fred Harvey's favor was that he always allowed customers sufficient time to eat, without disrupting train schedules. Twenty-five minutes may not seem like much time for breakfast, lunch or dinner, but with the organized, efficient Harvey service it was sufficient time to ensure enjoyment of the meal—and it was a far cry from the five or 10 minutes allowed at the dirty, crooked beaneries of days past. Split-second timing, with the participation of the train crews, was necessary to

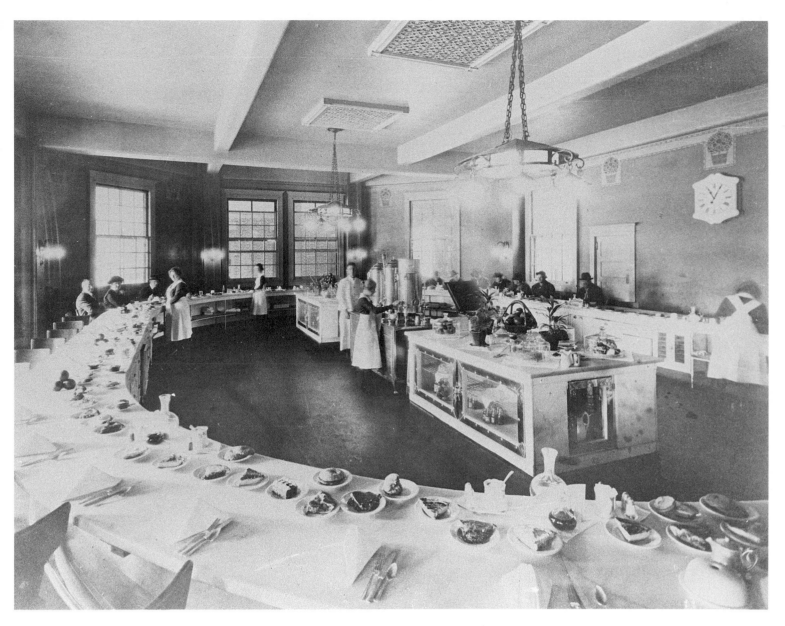

allow this phenomena of relatively leisurely eating on the railroad.

Before a meal stop, a brakeman went through the cars, asking passengers if they cared to dine, and if they wanted dining room or lunch-counter service. This information was wired ahead, so that the manager of the Harvey House would know how many people to expect and could plan the meal accordingly.

When the train was exactly one mile from the station, the engineer blew a signal on the whistle. An attendant—immaculately groomed, of course—stepped outside the restaurant and hit a gong once. At this sound, the waitresses placed the first course on the table. When the train stopped, the gong was hit several times and the passengers were seated. The later courses—steaks, ham and eggs, fish, chops and vegetables—were already cooking. After the first course, waitresses asked patrons what they preferred to drink—coffee, hot tea, iced tea or milk. They then placed the patron's cup in a special 'coded' position so that the Harvey Girl in charge of drinks would automatically know what to pour. If the cup was left right side up in its saucer, the patron was served coffee. An upside-down cup in the saucer called for hot tea. Upside-down and tilted against the saucer meant the customer wanted iced tea, and upside-down away from the saucer meant he wanted milk.

At 15 minutes to the train's departure, an attendant

gently told diners that there was no reason to hurry, there were still 15 minutes left. Time was called again at 10 minutes. Before the train departed, the conductor checked with the house manager to be certain all customers were finished eating and aboard the train. Only then did the Santa Fe cars continue on their way.

For all his service and hospitality, Fred Harvey demanded only one courtesy in return from his customers—that the gentlemen wear coats to the table. Waitresses were instructed to ignore occasional 'boors' who made scenes about the rule. Although Harvey offered sober alpaca jackets in assorted sizes to coatless patrons, his insistence on this, to him, essential element of polite dining caused him more trouble than he expected.

In Oklahoma, for instance, Chairman Campbell Russell of the State Corporation Commission stoutly maintained that coat-wearing was against Sooner custom. The Harvey House at Purcell thus refused to serve him. Russell and Harvey took the case all the way to the Supreme Court. After long deliberation, Harvey's position was upheld. The court reasoned that civilization in Oklahoma was in a precarious position as it was, and influences in its direction should be encouraged. Besides, the court stated, if Harvey were ordered to serve men without coats, what would follow? Orders to serve men without shirts, or only in breechclouts?

Cowhands also frequently demanded to be served coatless. In 1882, at the Castaneda, a newly-opened Harvey House in Las Vegas, New Mexico, some cowmen and their foreman rode into the dining room, shot off some bottlenecks, and, in loud and profane language, demanded a meal.

Fred Harvey was present, and not for a moment did he lose his poise. 'Gentlemen,' he said, stepping forward, 'ladies dine here. No swearing or foul language is permitted. You must leave quietly at once.'

They did, shamefacedly walking their horses from the room, carefully keeping the screen door from slamming behind them. The foreman later apologized for their behavior. To show there were no hard feelings, Harvey treated the cowpokes to a first-rate lunch—insisting, however, that his guests wear coats.

Only once was there an occasion recorded on which a brazen customer won his battle against the dinner jacket. In Dodge City in the 1920s, Mayor 'Big Bill' Thompson of Chicago—a formidable and forbidding figure—led some cowhands into the dining room of Harvey's El Vaquero hotel and demanded that they be served coatless.

Thompson was an intimidating man. He had recently challenged King George V to fight him barefisted in the Chicago Stadium. In any event, he got his cowhands fed, though the scornful glances of the Harvey Girls somewhat withered their bravado.

Harvey stopped at nothing to make his establishments' meals of both uniform quality and infinite variety. To provide consistently good coffee, for instance, he had the water at each of houses analyzed. Then he had special blends and mixtures developed to cancel out whatever effects the local water would have on the coffee's flavor.

Until Harvey added a little interest to menus, it was the custom to feed railroad passengers whatever was available locally from the region they were leaving. Passengers on trains out of Chicago got Lake Michigan whitefish and Illinois corn; in Kansas City, there were steaks; trains out of California were supplied with seafood and fruit. Harvey changed all that. He had the advantage of getting all freight service free from the Santa Fe. With the help of fast refrigerator cars—often run at the head of passenger trains—Chicagoans headed for the West Coast dined on California specialties before they got there; eastbound passengers got Kansas City steaks in the middle of the Mojave Desert.

The Harvey Company also cleaned up the act of the 'candy butchers'—candy sellers who walked from car to car aboard trains, offering snacks and reading materials. Harvey gave them good fiction and newspapers to sell, besides the cheap pulp fiction to which they had been limited. He also supplied them with higher-quality sweets. Sales rose impressively—by 1921, they were 60 times what they were when the Harvey Company was offered control of the service.

On top of all this, the Harvey Company was soon given the opportunity to branch out into the drug store business. It began with a drugstore at the new Union Station depot in Kansas City, and when this proved a great success, Harvey opened stores in Chicago, Cleveland, St Louis and Los Angeles.

But the company did not spread itself too thin. It was the very fact that the Harvey Company gave these stores as much attention as any giant hotel that made them a success. In 1921, Harvey's son told the story:

'When the new Union Station in Kansas City was about to be finished a few years ago, we were offered along with the restaurant and other concessions there, the chance to run the station drug store. If it had been a question of running an ordinary good drug store, we would not have been interested. We had never been in that business and we would not have cared to go into it for any such volume as we could have counted on.

'But when we looked into the possibilities of making it, in some respects at least, a more than ordinarily serviceable drug store, we were decidedly interested, and we took over the lease.

'We proceeded as nearly as possible in the spirit of the Florence Hotel. Take a minor line, like perfumery, for example. We stocked, in this railway station drug store, just about as comprehensive an assortment as you can find on State Street or Fifth Avenue or anywhere. There was no possibility of its paying its own way any time soon, and we did not expect it to—any more than the walnut furniture at Florence was expected to pay its extra cost soon.

'But we did expect it to please people. We expected it to make a good impression on them, not only for itself but for the rest of the store. We expected it to set them

talking about it and causing other people to come and see it. And after a while, on its own account, as well as by boosting sales in the rest of the store, we expected it to pay.

'And it certainly has not disappointed us. We do a larger business in this one, ordinarily, trifling line, I am told, than many prosperous drug stores altogether. Which is of course saying nothing of the effect on sales in the rest of the store, which has been considerable.

'We have not specialized in all lines to the same extent by any means but in every department of the store we have strived in some way to exceed the service expected, even though it could not be done at an immediate profit.

'The results have more than justified the policy. Before taking on the store, we got estimates from half a dozen experienced drug men on the volume we were likely to do. Our volume last year was six times as large as the largest of the estimates.'

When dining cars appeared, Harvey took charge of the Santa Fe's. Even though the kitchens were now moving

Above: **Fred Harvey's Casa del Desierto in Barstow, California—this building evidences that Harvey Hotels were the finest in the Southwest; meals, and the architecture and decor of Harvey facilities were unique but uniformly luxurious throughout the Santa Fe system.** *Below:* **The elaborate Harvey Hotel La Posada, in Winslow, Arizona.**

on wheels, the cuisine and service were of the same high Harvey standard. The pride and joy of the Santa Fe system was the dining car on the *California Limited,* an all first-class express between Chicago and Los Angeles, which laid on meals to rival those in the finest European hotels—for $1. A typical dinner on the *California Limited* consisted of eight courses: grapefruit; olives, salted almonds and radishes; consommé; filet of bass with cucumbers; lamb chops a la Nelson, with broiled fresh mushrooms; roast turkey with cranberry sauce, mashed potatoes and cauliflower; salad; and plum pudding, cakes, ice cream, cheese and/or fruit; and coffee. By the 1930s, faster trains had cut the need for railroad side stops, and two-thirds of Harvey service was in dining cars, although some houses were re-opened briefly during World War II.

The stewards of these cars were encouraged to take a personal interest in their establishments. Bill Gardner, for instance, steward on the Kansas City-Chicago run, devised a '1001 Dressing'—an improvement on Thousand Island dressing. If the passenger liked it, Gardner presented him or her with a personal card containing the recipe. This was exactly the kind of thing Harvey loved, and the kind of thing that gave his system its reputation.

It was kept up, too, after Harvey's death in 1901, by his sons. First Ford, then Byron (after Ford died in an aircraft accident in 1928), headed the Harvey system, trying never to waver from their father's standards.

In the early 1920s, for example, the bottom fell out of the cattle market, leaving many cattlemen—frequent Harvey patrons—smarting from their losses. They were most upset and resentful to find that Harvey restaurants had not lowered the prices for their roasts and steaks. They were getting less money for their cattle, they reasoned. Restaurants must be paying less money for their beef.

In fact, it was lower prices for beef by-products and cheap cuts of meat, which Harvey Houses never used, that drove down the price of cattle. The Harvey Company was paying as much as ever for fine steaks. But rather than lose the good will of so many of their customers, the Harvey system cut the prices of its roasts and steaks to the point where they made no profit on them at all—and kept cattlemen coming in. The move was considered well worth the temporary profit loss.

World War II made things difficult for the Harvey Company, as it did for many of those involved with the railroads. Food rationing, the necessary moving of thousands

of servicemen, much of the labor force going off to war—all of these factors could make even the most well-run system creak and strain. But the Harvey system saw it through. Many former Harvey Girls came out of retirement to help serve the trainloads of soldiers that descended from the cars three times a day. Byron Harvey, then head of the enterprise, placed a gentle ad in magazines and newspapers, explaining the difficulties to civilian patrons. The ad closed, 'Fred Harvey hospitality, like a lot of other good things, may be temporarily lacking. Thank you for understanding why and being so patient and good-humored about it. When this war is won we promise you again the Fred Harvey service you have learned to expect.'

In its nationwide ad campaign, the Harvey system also utilized the character of Private Pringle to explain the problems of wartime catering. Unknown to the ad developers, there really was a Private Pringle. His first name was Murray, and he wrote Byron Harvey that he 'liked the ads fine,' was now a corporal, and could Mr Harvey please get him a dinner date with Lana Turner when he got back to the States. The Harvey system promised to do its best, but there is no record of whether or not it succeeded.

In 1943, the Harvey system served over 30,000,000 meals, of which 8,000,000 were served to the armed forces. Food fed to travelers and soldiers included 512,000 pounds of coffee, making 20,480,000 cups; 662,000 pounds of butter; 1,117,000 gallons of milk and cream; 1,250,061 pounds of sugar; 2,412,400 pounds of flour; 4,616,400 pounds of potatoes; 956,840 pounds of fish; 2,493,595 pounds of poultry; 5,172,835 pounds of meat and 1,408,184 dozen eggs.

Wartime dining cars experienced as much of an increase in patronage as the Harvey Houses. On Santa Fe trains such as the *Scout* or *Ranger*, it was normal to feed 350 people in one 36-seat dining car, which meant the staff had to work through 10 30-minute seatings. At one breakfast on the *Scout*, the fry-cook fried 1004 consecutive eggs in one pan.

After the war, however, railroad passenger business began to drop off dramatically. The public's preference for flying or driving on the nation's new concrete network of highways 'ate into' even the Santa Fe's celebrated passenger service. The Fred Harvey Company was sold in 1968 to Amfac, Inc, a Hawaii-based corporation. Santa Fe passenger service was surrendered to Amtrak in 1973.

By the time it was sold, the Harvey Company owned some of the biggest, most beautiful hotels in the Southwest. The El Tovar for instance was, when it opened, one of the most expensive hotels in the country at $4 a day. It was also one of the most luxurious—built on the very rim of the Grand Canyon, and was more of a resort than a hotel. Nearby was Bright Angel, where small, cozy cottages and camping facilities could be had at lower prices. The Harvey subsidiary of Amfac, Inc still operates the hostelries and facilities around the Grand Canyon.

Some of the lovely Harvey Houses are now serving other uses. The elaborate La Posada at Winslow is now part of the Santa Fe divisional offices there. A Harvey House in Belen, New Mexico, is now a senior citizen center. These charming buildings are now what is left of an empire that once offered good welcome, good eating and good cheer to millions.

Opposite: The Fred Harvey Company's El Tovar Hotel, built on the rim of the Grand Canyon, is shown here in a vintage photo. *Above:* A Santa Fe passenger service ad boasting Fred Harvey meals.

A New Century

Built for Speed

The Santa Fe began the 20th century with a bang. Its passenger service was already famous for its comfort, speed and efficiency. But the company's handling of a millionaire miner's 1905 challenge to go from Los Angeles to Chicago faster than any railroad had ever gone before clinched its reputation, and was a small indicator of the technical advances, the speed and time records, to come in all fields between 1900 and the year 2000.

Persons who have a large surplus of ready money are privileged to indulge in fads and hobbies. One rich man collects rare paintings; another buys a yacht. John de Smyth, a famed early 20th century money man, spent a few millions for a big country estate; while Reginald van Rocks bought a new auto every month.

But until Walter Scott emerged into the limelight of publicity, no dollar-surfeited American ever had chartered a special train to travel two-thirds of the way across the continent 'just for the fun of it.'

About noon on Saturday, 8 July 1905, Scott, a heavily built man wearing a Stetson, walked into the office of Santa Fe's Los Angeles general passenger agent, J J Byrne.

'I'm Walter Scott, of Death Valley,' he said. 'Can you put me into Chicago in 46 hours?'

Yes, they certainly could, answered Byrne. For $5500.

Scott was told to be at the depot of La Grande Station the next day at 12:30 pm. The Santa Fe had his custom train, named the *Coyote Special* at his suggestion, ready and waiting. It consisted of baggage car 210, diner 1407, a Pullman observation car, *Muskegon,* and engine number 442, a 6-year old Baldwin 10-wheel 4–6–0. The first engineer on the run was Scotsman John Finlay.

At 12:47, Mr and Mrs Scott arrived at the depot in a limousine. Writer Charles Van Loan was waiting for them in the Pullman, and was already typing out a story for the newspapers. Santa Fe representative Frank Newton Holman was also on board.

Scott climbed onto the engine to shake hands with the engineer and the fireman. He then made a short speech to the crowd that had gathered and boarded the train.

There had been swift transcontinental runs to meet important business engagements, such as the hurried trip made over the Santa Fe in 1900 by Mr C R Peacock, Vice-President of the Carnegie Steel & Iron Co.

Sometimes because of sudden illness, fast trains had been chartered in a race from ocean to ocean, beating the regular *Limited* by many hours; such was the case when Mr H P Lowe, of the Engineering Company of America,

traveled from New York to Los Angeles, in 1903, using the special Santa Fe service west of Chicago.

It remained for 1905 to be made more famous as the year when Scott paid several thousand dollars for the privilege of riding from Los Angeles to Chicago faster than anybody else had ever made the trip.

Scott was quite a character. Born in Covington, Kentucky, he came West in his teens and occupied himself riding the range, 'trailing' cattle and even acting as a water boy for a government survey party in Death Valley. He toured as a trick rider with Buffalo Bill for 12 years, then established himself as a wealthy mine owner in Grapevine Canyon, above Death Valley. He was nicknamed Death Valley Scotty and he was obsessed with speed and spectacle.

As Scott briefly phrased it, 'I'm buying speed.' A shrewd journalist advanced another reason: 'Scott's not mad. It's just downright Western exuberance. He feels that the world is too small for the sort of whoop he wants to give.'

Whatever the reason, evidently he was satisfied with the bargain—though the average traveler was content with the fast time of the *California Limited,* which was scheduled to pick passengers up in Los Angeles at 1:10 pm one day and land them in Chicago at 11:15 am the third day out. That was fast enough traveling for the ordinary man of the time, requiring frequent spurts of a mile a minute on the long, level plains stretches to even up the slower pace while crossing the mountains.

In any case, conductor George Simpson gave the signal at 1:00 pm, July 9, and the *Coyote Special* slid out of the station on the first leg of its record-breaking trip to Chicago.

Crowds gathered by the side of the tracks day and night to see the train go by. At San Bernadino, a helper engine was used to make the run up Cajon Pass. Near the top, instead of stopping the train to take off the extra engine, as was the normal practice, a brakeman climbed to the back and uncoupled the engine, which simply sped off into a siding. Appropriate switches were thrown with split-second timing and the *Coyote Special* roared ahead, with no pause necessary. Never before had such a strategy to keep a train moving been tried.

On this trip, an 80-second engine change was considered slow. The train hit 96 miles per hour on the run to Barstow, passing between mileposts 44 and 43 in 39

At right: **Two boys examine, in amazement, the giant running gear of Santa Fe steam loco 2925, shown here as a museum piece.** *Overleaf:* **A modern remake of the** *Coyote Special.* **Engine Number 1010, used on the original train, is now at the Railroad Museum in Sacramento.**

seconds. Fred Jackson, the engineer on the twist-filled run near Needles, got a little carried away and took the curves at 65 miles per hour. The jarring dumped the party's just-begun dinner to the floor.

This was unfortunate, because on this auspicious occasion, the Santa Fe felt obliged to more than live up to its reputation for fine food. The train's private chef, a Mr Geyer, had provided caviar sandwiches, iced consomme, porterhouse steak, broiled squab, ice cream and french coffee.

With Van Loan dropping off frequent dispatches for the Associated Press, the high-speed train ride was soon front-page news all over the country. Interest in the *Coyote Special* mounted, and the crowds lining the tracks grew hourly.

Scott did not forget to reward the train crews personally. A few miles before the end of each leg of the journey, he would climb out onto the tender and slide down the cab of the locomotive to give $20 gold pieces to the engineer, fireman and division superintendent, who usually rode along at the head end.

The 536, an Atlantic-type 4–4–2 locomotive, was used east of La Junta until the *Coyote* reached Syracuse. For the Syracuse to Dodge run, the Santa Fe chose the 531. At Dodge, Scott sent a telegram to President Theodore Roosevelt:

'An American cowboy is coming east on a special train faster than any cowpuncher ever rode before stop how much shall I beat the record query.'

Roosevelt, perhaps wisely, did not commit himself.

The Santa Fe did itself proud. Not merely because the Scott Special made the fastest time between the two points named—for that only lowered a long-distance record already belonging to the Santa Fe—but mainly because the phenomenal run was made under normal conditions of track, motive power, and equipment, and practically on a moment's notice. No racing machines were used. The locomotives were the plain, everyday kind, taken from regular runs and manned by employees taking their regular turn. To be sure, the main line was

Above: **The Pullman sleeper,** *Santa Helena,* **evidencing one of its two retractable 'vestibules' by which passengers could walk from car to car.** *Below right:* **The Santa Fe's** *Grand Canyon* **passes a freight train at Cajon Pass, where the main line breaches the coastal mountains.**

kept clear, and even the exclusive *California Limited* put on the side track. The Scott Special had the right-of-way. That was the only favor shown it, though the engineers understood they had permission to 'let her out a few notches,' and they did so, when they could with safety.

Viewed from behind the scenes the run was as thrilling as any drama of the stage. In the dispatcher's office the operator would hardly have time to put one 'OS' on the sheet before another would be handed him over the wire. As one of the division superintendents laconically remarked, 'It looked as though the train were falling down a well.'

In making the schedule it was strung up so that the train was an hour late, to enable engineers to reach out after the time—which they all did—and to enable the opposing trains to move without delay—which they all did.

Everybody was keyed up to the highest tension, and it was a relief to each superintendent when the special left his division. Section gangs, with the fast schedule in hand, carefully walked the track half an hour before 'Scotty' and his flyer were due, inspecting rails, ties, and culverts. Switches and frogs were closely examined. Each man did his duty, which is why complete success resulted. As General Manager Hurley, of the line east of Albuquerque, said to a newspaper reporter, 'It makes me proud of the men who did the work; there was not a hitch; no one stuck his head out at the wrong time; not a switch was misplaced.' It was Hurley who wired the following dispatch to his men:

'I congratulate and compliment the operating and mechanical departments upon the unprecedented handling of the Scott Special. It indicates competent, careful supervision and management. I thank all interested for their splendid work.'

Record after record was broken. The final one was reached between Cameron and Surrey, Illinois, when 2.8

miles were run in 95 seconds, a rate of 106 miles per hour. This was a world record. Veteran Santa Fe engineer Charles Losee had control of the 510 engine from Fort Mason to Chillicothe, and used it to make the 105 mile run in 101 minutes.

The train pulled into the Dearborn Street station at 11:54 on 11 July—44 hours and 45 minutes after it left La Grande, 2267 miles away. The trip had required 19 engines and eight engine crews. The engines used were two Rhode Island 10-wheelers; one Baldwin 10-wheeler; four Baldwin Prairies; three Baldwin Pacifics; and nine Baldwin Atlantics.

A few days later, Scott and his wife took the *California Limited* home. In this day of jet travel, with the trip from Los Angeles to Chicago taking an average of three hours, the achievement of Scott and the Santa Fe doesn't seem like much. But at the time, it was considered a miracle of modern technology—and boded well for the passenger service of the Santa Fe.

World War I

With the outbreak of World War I in 1914 and the US intervention in the war in 1917 came one of the most problematic times for American railroads in history. It was marked by an only partially successful takeover of the railways by the federal government brought on by nagging labor disputes.

Labor unions had been growing in strength since the beginning of the 20th century, much to the chagrin of Santa Fe President Edward Ripley, a staunch opponent of organized labor. He believed instead that workers and the company should join together in team work and cooperation. He expected sacrifices from his workers for the good of the company and, like any manager, wanted to keep operating costs as low as possible. Ideally, employees would then be treated well by a benevolent management. Ripley did, in fact, establish death benefit programs for employees' families, accomodations and facilities—such as some luxuriously outfitted YMCAs, which the Santa Fe helped finance—for crewmen and workers along the rails, and other valuable perks. But he was horrified by the Adamson Bill, passed in 1916, establishing an eight-hour day for most railway workers—so much so that he declined to give the traditional Christmas bonuses to those employees covered by the new law. In 1914 he wrote:

'...the threatening attitude of the labor organizations must not be lost sight of.... Your company has always shown the utmost consideration for its employees, and as a class they are a credit to themselves and the road. Left to themselves there would be little of which to complain, but the organizations as a body have been aggressively demanding increased wages for their members with no regard for the ability of their employers to pay, and have been steadily demanding, and frequently with success, many varieties of legislation, such as full-crew bills, designed to increase operating expenses.'

The unions, however, felt that their demands were justified. The 'benevolent management' ideal was, after all, not nearly as widespread a reality as Ripley liked to think it was. Strikes became more frequent and more hostile.

After the outset in Europe of World War I in 1914, railways had to cope with increased sales of munitions and

Above: **A side view of the fireman's station of a huge steam loco.** *Below left:* **The engineer's station aboard same—the handle at above right is the throttle.** *Below right:* **A Santa Fe livestock car.**

foodstuffs to the European Allies. The railway network carried giant shipments to ports on the Atlantic and the Gulf. When the United States entered the War on 17 April 1917, the volume of goods and personnel shipped to Eastern ports became massive. A critical shortage of cars arose. Bottlenecks multiplied. Traffic increased 30 percent in 1916, 43 percent in 1917. The strain on the railways reached emergency levels. The American Railway Association had tried to draft a plan for coping with such potential problems in 1915, but it had never expected traffic jams like the ones that now occurred on the East Coast.

With the war came inflation, and the railroad unions demanded cost-of-living increases. The threat of a national railway strike, the last thing the nation or any of the roads could afford, loomed large on the horizon. Available shipping from the ports became rarer. Chaos reigned at the oceanside terminals.

President Woodrow Wilson took action. He had no intention of allowing the United States rail system to be paralyzed by a strike or anything else. At noon on 28 December 1917, the president took control of the rail system under the Federal Possession and Control Act. A Railway Control Act to provide for payment so that stockholders would be protected was instituted 1 March 1918. The US Railroad Administration, or USRA, operated the system, repaired equipment, maintained the tracks and paid compensation equal to the average net operating income during the previous three years ending 30 June 1917. It was agreed that the railroad companies would be returned to their respective owners within 21 months after the end of all wartime hostilities.

The USRA reorganized the US railway network and coordinated the traffic flow. The Santa Fe was well represented within the Administration. Secretary of the Treasury William G McAdoo was appointed its director general, with Walter D Hines, a former chairman of the Santa Fe board of directors, as assistant director general. Edward Chambers, a former Santa Fe vice president, became the director of the division of traffic while Ford Harvey, eldest son of Fred Harvey and now in charge of all Harvey operations, served as an advisor on dining facilities.

As it happened, McAdoo's duties as secretary of the Treasury kept him occupied, leaving Hines largely responsible for the day-to-day running of the Administration. He eventually succeeded McAdoo as director general. During this experience, Hines, formerly an opponent of government intervention in the railroads' affairs, became a strong supporter of public regulation paired with private ownership of the railroads. He was interested in establishing as a national priority the creation of a coordinated federal rail policy for the protection of investors, workers and shipping customers, but during the war there were few resources and a little time to spend on developing such a plan.

The USRA's running of the Santa Fe produced uneven results. Although Ripley remained the actual president of the Atchison Topeka & Santa Fe, William Benson Storey became the company's 'federal' manager. Off-line offices closed. Ticket agencies of several railroads were consolidated into one. Under government directives to maximize efficiency, each railroad routed traffic over lines owned by their former competitors, and shippers were not allowed to designate specific routes. Terminal operations were combined, and railroads frequently had to repair equipment belonging to other lines. This was hard on the Santa Fe, whose maintenance costs rose from $22.7 million in 1916 to $46 million in 1919 and $58.4 million in 1920. Losses began to mount as all other considerations besides the actual moving of men and materials were put aside.

In 1917, despite the incredible volume of traffic, railroad profits either failed to rise or actually declined. Ripley, along with other railway leaders, asked the ICC to allow higher rates. In June of 1918, the USRA raised rates 28 percent for freight and 18 percent for passengers. But this rate increase could not cover the cost of substantial increases in wages and taxes paid by the railroads.

The USRA's pay scales and rules, which have been described as 'featherbedding,' caused the cost of labor to skyrocket. The cost of living had risen 40 percent between 1915 and 1917, necessitating raising the average wage of railroad workers from $828 to $1004 per year. The USRA's Railroad Wage Commission discovered that 51 percent of railroad workers earned $75 per month or less and that 80 percent earned $100 per month or less. The Administration then introduced a new sliding scale for wages which provided retroactive pay increases from 1 January 1918. On 25 May 1918, the average wage was raised on order of McAdoo. It reached $1485 in 1919 and $1820 in 1920. The USRA also worked closely with the railroad labor unions, negotiating blanket contracts which for the first time rendered the Santa Fe almost totally unionized.

The government levied a corporate income tax of two percent, a war income tax of four percent and an excess

profits tax. State taxes also increased. The Santa Fe's federal tax bill alone rose from $862,334 in 1916 to $4.8 million in 1917. State taxes for the company went from $5.9 million to $7.1 million. The total increase in taxes in that year was $5.2 million, or an amount equal to almost 20 percent of the Santa Fe's net operating revenue.

The USRA agreed to pay a rental fee of $43.9 million to the Santa Fe to compensate it for use of the system. The railroad still lost much potential revenue that there would never be any way of replacing. According to the *Wall Street Journal*, the Santa Fe would have earned 8.35 percent in 1919 if it had been operated under its own management. Under federal management, the net operating income declined steadily instead. Even so, the USRA's running of the Santa Fe was considered successful relative to its operation of other roads. Its costs only slightly outweighed its intake on the Santa Fe. On the whole, though, the experiment of federalizing the railroads during wartime was considered less than successful by everyone involved.

After the war ended, traffic and earnings declined sharply. The USRA was no longer a convenience, it certainly wasn't profitable, and Wilson wanted an end to the federalization. Thus the railroads were returned to their owners 1 March 1920. The railroads, smarting from their losses, demanded fiscal adjustments for USRA operations. In response, Congress passed the Transportation Act of 1920, ensuring for the railroads an income of not less than half the previous rate during the first six months following termination of federal control. The railroads were not happy with this proposal, and adjustments were made, with the Santa Fe receiving a check for $21.5 million in 1922.

Labor demanded a continuation of its gains after the war, and the most part held on to those gains, although there were some bitter experiences, especially during the 1920s. The Transportation Act set up a nine-member Railroad Labor Board to hear labor disputes. A 22 percent wage increase was granted by the board in 1920, but revenues fell in 1921 and there was a 12 percent wage reduction. There were more strikes. One was disastrous and bitter. Shopmen struck, and another company union replaced them. Crewmen joined the strikers, stranding 3000 passengers in Arizona and California. The strike finally ended with the help of the Labor Board, but labor-management relations were in shreds.

The economy of the Southwest began to grow in the 1920s, and the ICC stepped in with new principles and guidelines. Tensions eased. Directors Henry Clay Frick and Augustus Julliard died in 1919, Ripley in 1920. These men, despite their merit, were '19th century' railroad men, with tried and true ideas that were sometimes unable to respond to the modern pressures around them in a way that reflected the period. William Benson Storey, a California native, University of California graduate and former surveyor and engineer, succeeded Ripley as president. With young, fresh '20th century' executives, Storey and his company expanded agricultural and industrial operations. The Santa Fe was ready for what lay ahead.

At right: Santa Fe Depot in Los Angeles, in the early 20th century. Note the unusual architecture, the elaborate entryway and the vintage autos—which were harbingers of doom for passenger service, and yet the World Wars absolutely stuffed stations like this with passengers.

A Step Ahead

by Thomas York

Passenger Trains

For nearly 100 years, the Santa Fe set the national standard for comfort, luxury and speed in passenger service. It also established records for rapid freight deliveries for commercial and industrial customers.

The Santa Fe created a standard for passenger train service that was matched by few American railroads. For example, the New York Central's *Twentieth Century Limited*, a name that became synonymous with luxury and prestige, was equally matched by Santa Fe's *Super Chief*—the first all-diesel, all-Pullman streamliner in the United States.

Introduced in 1937, *The Super Chief* sped between Chicago and Los Angeles in 39.5 hours, which was more than 14 hours faster than its steam predecessor, *The Chief*. *The Super Chief* became known for its luxury and food and, in the 1940s and 1950s, was the train for the rich and famous.

Santa Fe was not the first railroad to use diesels for passenger service, but it was the first to take advantage of diesel power plants for streamlined passenger service from the Midwest to the West Coast. The first prototype General Motors diesel engines were used to generate power for the Chevrolet assembly line at the Century of Progress exhibition in Chicago in 1933.

Although extremely experimental, diesels attracted the attention of the Burlington Railroad, which was seeking a revolutionary new train to attract passengers lost to the automobile. Burlington pursuaded GM to make one of the engines available for its new train. Despite reluctance on the part of GM, the engine and the experimental train proved successful and the age of the diesel locomotive was born.

The original *Super Chief* featured two twin-diesel locomotives built by the Electromotive Corporation, a General Motors subsidiary at La Grange, Illinois. The locomotives, each rated at 3600 horsepower, were constructed in two units and were tested in different terrain and conditions before they were delivered to the Santa Fe. When the twin locomotives were put to the test hauling a nine-car Pullman, they broke the record set in 1905 by the Santa Fe steam locomotive, the *Coyote Special*.

With the test completed, the results were conclusive—diesel locomotives were here to stay. All that was needed was a sturdier trackbed to support the high-flyer passenger train. Santa Fe spent $4 million improving the tracks and the roadbed between Los Angeles and Chicago before putting *The Super Chief* into day-to-day service.

In the days of Santa Fe passenger service, the famous *Super Chief (above)* ascends the grade near the old Dick Wooton Ranch at Wooton, Colorado. *At right:* Meals served on the Santa Fe's dining cars were intended to be the best for a modest price, in the Harvey tradition.

The diesel engines of the two locomotives proved they were better than steam engines and could operate at higher speeds for longer distances without expensive water stops along the way. Such water stops were required by steam locomotives, especially in desert climates.

The entire train was constructed of stainless steel, with sleepers from the Pullman Company and with club, baggage, dining and lounge cars constructed by the Budd Company. The cars were named after the Indian pueblos: Isleta, Laguna, Acoma, Cochiti, Oraibi, Taos and Navajo. With a full passenger manifest, the train carried 104 people, not including the train crew and eight postal clerks.

The second *Super Chief* unit also featured nine cars, giving Santa Fe twice-a-week service between Chicago and the West Coast. In the later 1930s, five-car trains were added to the streamliner service, giving Santa Fe 13 streamliners, which was more than any other railroad in the US.

The first diesels did not have quite the charm of the Santa Fe's *De Luxe*, a six-car passenger steam train that carried 70 passengers on its first run in 1911. This train featured two drawing room cars, an observation car, a

The photo of Santa Fe's *Navajo* passenger liner *at right* gives us a
view of passengers relaxing in the 'out-of-doors' amid rugged Western
scenery. *Above:* A Santa Fe passenger service anti-aircraft ad.

dining car and a club car as well as showers, tub baths, electric hair-styling irons and a fiction library. Its crew included a ladies' maid, a barber, a manicurist and a hairdresser. The extra fare to take advantage of this service was $25, and the *De Luxe* took 63 hours to make the 2267-mile run.

Many railroads, including the Santa Fe, prided themselves on their dining car service—even though most dining cars lost money. They were operated as loss leaders, with the expectation that excellent food and service would draw passengers from competing lines. The theory worked to the advantage of the Santa Fe and Fred Harvey. The Santa Fe made money on its passenger service with reliable service and good food.

For a time, the Santa Fe tried to cooperate with the coming of air travel. In 1929, the railroad pioneered cross-country service via the New York Central and Universal Air Lines, as well as with the Pennsylvania Railroad and Transconinental Air Transport. Passengers boarded a train in New York, then took an airplane from the Midwest to the Southwest. There they boarded a Santa Fe train bound for Los Angeles. The trip took three nights and two days. The service continued long enough for better passenger planes to come into service, thus rendering the train connections obsolete.

Throughout the early days of railroading, few improvements were made to dining cars. George Pullman had

Above: **These happy folks are enjoying the service aboard a Santa Fe club car, in the 'roaring' 1920s.** *At right:* **An ad, circa 1951, for the sophisticated pleasures of the *Super Chief's* Turquoise Room service.**

taken out the original patents in 1865 for cars in which passengers could sit and eat. But it was not until 1925 that the Santa Fe put its own design in service in hopes of creating an advantage over its rail competitors. A two-car set placed at the front of passenger trains included a diner and club lounger, with bath, barber shop and soda fountain, and held 42 customers in the diner alone. The trains also featured sleeping and shower facilities for the crew.

When the diesel proved its value in passenger service, Santa Fe officials set about replacing its freight service fleet of steam locomotives. The Electromotive Corporation delivered a 5400-horsepower engine to the railroad in 1938 nicknamed *The Jeep* and given the number 100. *The Jeep* hauled its first train of 68 freight cars from Kansas City to Los Angeles under regular operating conditions, and proved that it could haul more freight cars up a grade at a higher speed than any steam locomotive in service at the time. No 100 trimmed the time it took a freight train to traverse the distance from Chicago to Los Angeles from six to four days and then three days. In 1938, hauling a train from the Great Lakes to the West Coast by steam required nine engines and a total of 35 stops for fuel and water. No 100, on the other hand, required just five stops.

Welcome to the
Turquoise Room

the only private dining room in the world on rails

aboard the new Super Chief

TURQUOISE ROOM

Santa Fe

Entertain in the grand manner while en route between Chicago and Los Angeles — in a perfectly appointed private dining room for a party up to ten.

The Turquoise Room in the new Lounge Car of the new Super Chief is the most distinctive social feature ever provided on any train.

You are invited to enjoy it, and the other new features on the beautiful new all-room Super Chief. For Turquoise Room reservations, just consult any Santa Fe ticket agent, or the dining-car steward on the Super Chief

Diesel power plants were unique. Instead of one big steam plant, each diesel unit held four 900-horsepower diesel motors which generated current to drive eight traction motors directly connected to the truck axles. If problems developed in one of the two diesel units, the other unit would continue to produce power, allowing the diesels to run continuously for long periods without major delays. On the other hand, if steam engines experienced trouble they were forced to shut down, and sometimes entire trains had to be halted until repairs could be made.

In addition, steam locomotives were available for just one-third of their operating lives, with the other two-thirds spent in repairs (although many roundhouse mechanics managed to keep some steam locomotives operating 60 percent of the time). Diesels, however, could be in service 95 percent of the time.

With the introduction of diesel locomotives in the 1930s, the Santa Fe pioneered the changeover for passenger and freight operations. In 1935 it was the first railroad to use diesels, which pulled its famed *Super Chief* streamlined passenger trains from Chicago to Los Angeles and which continued to set the pace for passenger service over the next three decades.

The *Super Chief*, one of the best-known passenger trains in the world, was used extensively by Hollywood motion picture stars and other celebrities. It succeeded *The Chief,* an all-steam train that ran between the 'Windy City' and Los Angeles beginning in 1923. The all-Pullman *Super Chief* was followed by *El Capitan,* an all-coach streamlined diesel train inaugurated between Los Angeles and Chicago in 1938.

Soon after the introduction of diesels in the 1930s, the fastest runs in the United States for both freight and passenger service were achieved by the new locomotives, and the days of steam were numbered. By 1943 two Santa Fe operating divisions were completely diesel, and by 1959 the last steam locomotives had been retired from the fleet.

The Santa Fe had established its reputation for fast, reliable and comfortable passenger service long before the arrival of The *Super Chief.* For example, Edward Ripley was given credit for establishing The *California Limited*—for years, one of the best known trains from the Midwest to the West Coast. It was an all-Pullman train, and all passengers had to purchase tickets. No free passes were allowed, not even for Ripley. Whenever he rode the train, he presented his ticket to the conductor just like the other passengers.

The *Limited* was extremely popular in the summer months when people were headed to and from California. Each day as many as seven trains, each containing 11 sleeping cars filled with passengers, left Dearborn Station in Chicago or Union Station in Los Angeles within a half hour of each other. At one point, no fewer than 45 trains operated between the two cities—a record never broken.

The 45 trains—22 eastbound and 23 westbound—operated over the tracks simultaneously. During the three-day run, each train used a minimum of 15 locomotives with 15 train crews. For more than 10 years, The *California Limited* was the grandest and most popular train in the world.

Not all Santa Fe passenger accommodations, however, were so luxurious as to prohibit the everyday American from using them. The Santa Fe also, beginning in 1905, offered a 'tourist class' sleeping car at reduced rates. They got from Chicago to California just as fast as the first-class Pullmans (they were usually part of the same train), stopped at the same Harvey houses, passed through the same scenery. They even had a small 'Baker oven' built

Left: An early 1950s ad for the *El Capitan.* The *El Capitan* (at Raton Pass, *above right*) came to incorporate the 'Hi-Level' scenic view cars shown here. *Below:* This lady adjusts the 'climate' controls in her early 1950s Santa Fe sleeper unit. *Opposite:* Amtrak passenger service.

onto the car's hot water heater. All they lacked were the plush upholstery and elaborately carved woodwork of the first-class cars. Even without these luxuries, tourist class cars were immeasurably more pleasant than the 'immigrant trains,' which offered only wooden benches (bedding was supplied by the sleeper) for their passengers. As such, they were immensely popular with the middle class, once the Santa Fe had convinced its potential customers that to ride tourist class was respectable.

Even though the Santa Fe offered the best passenger service in the world, however, it too eventually succumbed to the popularity of the personal automobile and the passenger plane. The Santa Fe surrendered its passenger service to Amtrak in 1973.

Freight Innovations

While the Santa Fe was guarding its reputation for passenger service, it was also upgrading the size and speed of its freight locomotives. By 1911, the Santa Fe shops had built some of the largest steam locomotives ever constructed.

In one case, two engines were constructed from four older locomotive 2–8–0s. These engines, 2–8–8–0 Mallets, were followed by the construction of two big engines constructed for passenger service with a wheel arrangement of 4–4–6–0. They were used for six years, then rebuilt.

Baldwin also brought out two huge Mallets with a wheel arrangement of 2–8–8–2, which Santa Fe later reconstructed into four 2–8–2 types. The quest for size

ended in 1911 when Santa Fe built 10 Mallets with a wheel arrangement of 2–10–10–2. They were the largest in the world but, despite their tractive power of 111,600 pounds, were unsuccessful and were later rebuilt into smaller 2–10–2 units.

Santa Fe designers wanted Baldwin to give the 'super locomotive' concept one more shot, with the construction of a quadruplex, double compound Mallet 2–8–8–8–8–2. The boiler was to have been flexible, with a joint in the middle, and with two cabs, one in front and one in back. It would have weighed more than 442 tons and would have had a tractive power of 220,000 pounds, but it was never built.

Troubled Times

The Great Depression

The 1920s have gone down in history as an age of prosperity. But even before the stock market crash in 1929, there were signs that the American and European economies were not as healthy as they appeared. Profits in agriculture lagged far behind those to be made in the industrial sector. Some individual industries, as well as many European countries, had never recovered from the recession that put in an appearance after World War I. There was so much speculation in the stock market that little money was invested in public works or manufacturing plants.

But between 24 and 29 October, 1929, the cracks in the so-called 'Coolidge Prosperity' became painfully evident to all. The stock market crashed, ruining investors and businesses and putting millions out of their jobs.

At first, it seemed that the Santa Fe would hardly be touched by this national catastrophe. The economy had slowed down, but had not stopped moving forward completely. The Southwest seemed far away from the problems on Wall Street. The railroad operated normally for a few months. Then, in 1930, drought turned a huge part of the area served by the Santa Fe into a near-wasteland. Thousands of square miles of once-fertile farm and cattle land became the 'Dust Bowl.' With no grain and little livestock to ship, the Santa Fe suffered the worst traffic losses in history. The railroad had to take action.

Emergency rates on feed and cattle were introduced, to help get livestock out of the Dust Bowl and save that which remained. Dividends on stock were lowered, then disappeared altogether.

Immediately after the crash, President Herbert Hoover asked the nation's industries to try to maintain their projected capital spending outlays and to keep employment levels steady. The Santa Fe did its best to cooperate. It announced in its 1929 *Annual Report* that it would spend $85 million for 5854 new freight cars and 49 new passenger cars. It had no intention of abandoning the 172 miles of track it had under construction at the time, and anticipated building 380 miles more. However, in June of 1930, this optimism faltered. Shop and maintenance crews were reduced, although the orders for new equipment held. William Storey, president of the Santa Fe during the early part of the Depression, asked that Santa Fe employees accept a 10 percent cut in wages. In this way, he hoped to prevent additional layoffs and keep the railroad's employment level steady. Company officers and labor union officials agreed to the reduction. Though the Santa Fe's total mileage peaked in 1932, the next year saw the abandonment of 126 miles of less frequently used track.

Among the companies that made a go of it during the Depression, the Santa Fe was relatively strong, steady and secure. Confidence in the company was high. Storey declared many times that maintenance programs would be kept up on all property and that the company had no intention of letting any of it deteriorate. The wage cut was extended; but this, again, was for the purpose of keeping

Below: One of the chief breadwinners of the Santa Fe, the boxcar.
Right: A passenger train passes through the arid West of the 1930s.
Overleaf: The Chicago Exposition of 1938 produced this contrast between state of the art steam (second to left) and diesel power.

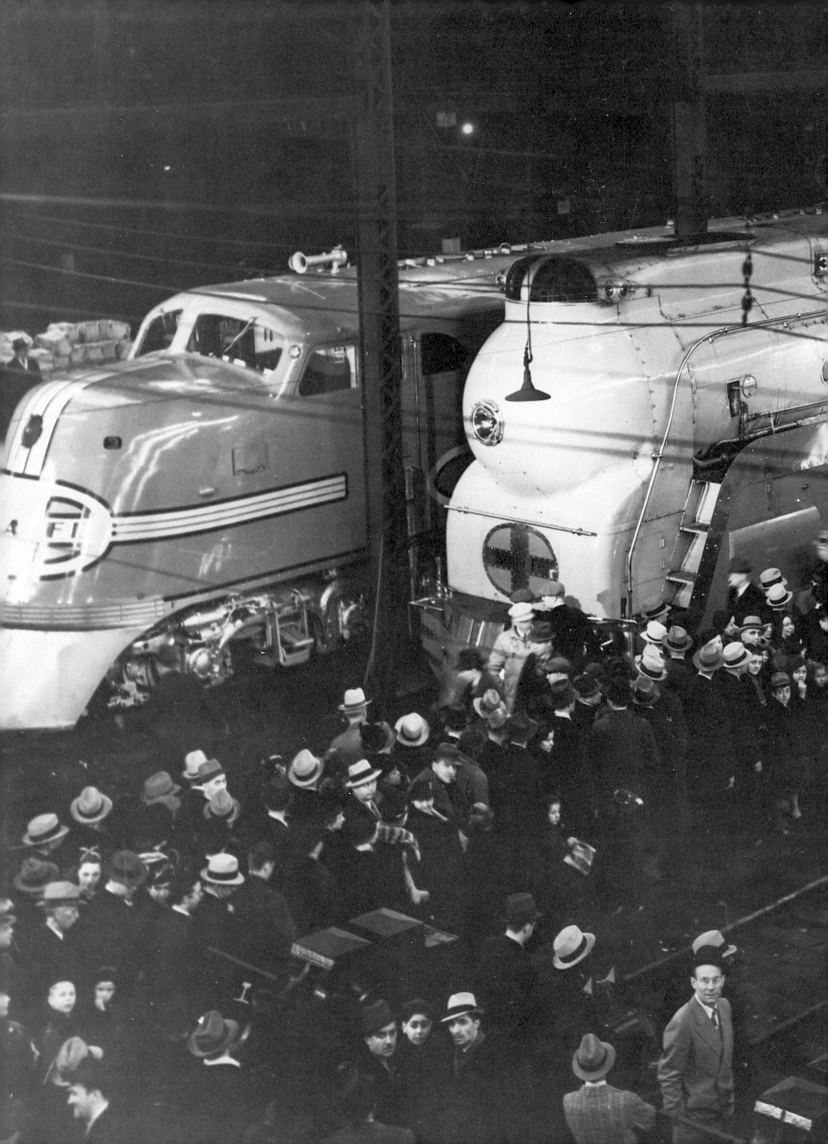

Not even such an advanced steam loco as the Santa Fe's *Blue Goose* (left) could prevent the age of diesels, though mighty were such steamers as the 2–8–8–2 shown *above* helping the *Chief* up Raton Pass.

as many Santa Fe workers employed as possible. Capital spending fell to only $2.5 million, and coach passenger rates were slashed to 2 cents per mile to attract business. Storey did well in keeping his company's head above water.

The pressures on him, however, were considerable. Storey retired in 1933, and was succeeded by Samuel Bledsoe, to whom it remained to see the Santa Fe safely through the Great Depression.

A lawyer, Bledsoe had already served as chairman of the executive committee and general counsel for the railroad. He had been a leading spokesman for the Santa Fe, and the rail industry in general, before the Interstate Commerce Commission and various Congressional committees. He seemed a natural choice for president.

But there was something different about this president. Unlike Strong, Ripley and Storey, Bledsoe was not a 'railroadman'—that is, he had not worked his way up through the ranks, starting as a clerk or telegraph operator. He came to the railroad and his position through his practice of law.

Bledsoe was born in Kentucky on 12 May 1868. He studied law at the University of Texas and worked in Indian and Oklahoma territories, becoming a specialist in

land and railroad affairs. He got a job representing the Santa Fe in Ardmore in 1895, and eventually became the company's general attorney for Oklahoma. His work was considered outstanding. He was appointed as the general counsel for the railroad, and then obtained various other executive positions.

Despite his lack of experience in the more 'hands-on' aspects of railroading, such as laying track, surveying and engineering, Bledsoe was knowledgeable about the system and accepted innovations and changes in marketing and technology. It was under him that the Santa Fe purchased diesel locomotives for all types of service, streamlined its passenger trains, and instituted new approaches to the marketing of transportation. Last but not least, of course, Bledsoe steered the company through the Depression well.

Bledsoe continued the cost-saving practices instituted by Storey. More track was abandoned, mostly in Oklahoma, Texas and New Mexico. A new branch, however, was opened. It was in the Pecos Valley leading to a United States Potash factory, and it brought in much additional traffic. Net income in 1934 was double what it had been the year before, and though the Santa Fe was still in for some ups and downs, income never again fell as low as it had been in 1933. A common stock dividend of 2 percent was declared. Money allocated for capital improvements increased, as did earnings. In a major victory for

74

Above: **This 1947 model refrigerator or 'reefer' car was a big advance over previous models, with its 'modern' design—still, note the ice hatches on top.** *Below opposite:* **The Harvey hotel El Navajo in Gallup.**

Bledsoe, the 10 percent employee wage cut was revoked on 1 April 1935, costing the company $6,150,000.

By now, railroads had to worry not only about losing business due to the Depression, but also about competition from the trucking and pipeline industries. To combat this problem, Bledsoe speeded up schedules and improved service, spending almost $4 million to superelevate problematic curves between Chicago and Los Angeles and lay 140 miles of new 112-pound rail.

The trucking industry had been unable to grow earlier because of a lack of good highways in the United States. The truckers' first inroad into the railway industry's territory was in the transport of 'less than carload' lots or 'LCL' shipments.These had always been a dependable commodity for the Santa Fe. In 1931, as one way of combatting the trucking competition, the Santa Fe began to offer pickup and delivery service for LCL shipments. This did not provide enough of an edge to the company to give it an advantage over truckers. Thus, under Bledsoe's direction in 1935, the Santa Fe bought controlling interest in a bus and truck operator, the Southern Kansas Stage Line. In 1939, the Santa Fe bought the remaining part of Southern Kansas securities. It also bought up other trucking outfits in the area. The Santa Fe Trail Transportation Company, a new subsidiary, was introduced. It worked with the railroad, both divisions coordinating their efforts to provide door-to-door service to LCL customers. Eventually, the operation was extended west through Arizona and California. It added new diesel cabs to pull sleek, stainless steel trailers.

During World War II, the total mileage of the trucking routes grew to 7300; by 1949, it was 9444. There were federal regulations limiting the trucking line to only those areas already reached by the Santa Fe rails, but the coordinated railway-highway service proved profitable.

Profits declined a bit from 1936 to 1937, but total revenues increased. Things were looking up, and Bledsoe elected to continue expansion. He placed a $19.6 million order for 155,000 tons of rail, several of a new type of light-weight passenger car, 27 locomotives, and more than 3000 freight cars. This was the largest order since the beginning of the Depression.

In 1931, the Santa Fe had begun to build a new stretch of track from Amarillo, Texas through Boise City, Oklahoma to Las Animas, Colorado. Construction gangs only got as far as Boise City before the Depression and the Dust Bowl stopped them dead. The railroad still needed the line, however, and in 1936 when economic conditions improved it began work to cover the 111 miles between Boise City and Las Animas. This was the largest stretch of new railroad constructed since the beginning of the Depression, and it cost the Santa Fe $3.75 million. The line opened 1 February 1937, making it part of a route from Amarillo to Denver that was the shortest in the nation by 25 miles. The governor of Colorado himself participated in the opening ceremonies, riding a special train to Springfield, Colorado to drive in a 'golden spike.' The completion of this line proved the acute foresight of the leaders of the Santa Fe. When prosperity finally returned to the beleaguered Dust Bowl, followed by the revitalization of the farming and cattle industries and the discovery of oil in the area, the Amarillo-Las Animas Cutoff proved a solid investment and a lucrative route.

Despite the problems of the Depression, the Santa Fe had faith in the Texas area and its potential for growth. It tried to consolidate and strengthen its network there during the 1930s. In 1937, it bought a 215-mile branch line from the St Louis-San Francisco Railroad, also known as the 'Frisco,' which was in severe financial trouble. The route, which ran from Fort Worth through Brownwood to Menard, was not profitable for the Frisco, but the Santa Fe had a use for it as a shortcut from Fort Worth to the Coleman Cut-off at Brownwood. Acquisition of the line reduced the journey from Fort Worth to California by 117 miles. The Frisco was paid $1.5 million for the property, which was in need of renovation and had on it obligations of more than $15 million. Work on the route was started 2 May 1937, when the Santa Fe officially took possession of it. It was soon a heavily loaded, profitable line—and the Santa Fe had gotten it for a song because of the low Depression prices.

About this time, Bledsoe launched an energetic advertising campaign to solicit business to help pay for the building and improvements. The Santa Fe, beginning in 1937, placed full-page ads in *Fortune, Time, News-Week, Nation's Business* and *States News.* They were unusual in that they were freight ads independent of those soliciting passenger business. This campaign, coupled with a good harvest, helped to make 1937 the most successful year since 1931. Even passenger traffic showed improvement.

In 1938, however, the government reduced some expenditures which had been helping the American economy to limp back to its feet. The economy slowed again, and the Santa Fe again had to refrain from issuing common stock dividends. A slight improvement came in 1939.

This was a strenuous time for Bledsoe, who was particularly concerned about the hardships of Santa Fe employees and their families during this troubled period. He fell ill, then died on 8 March 1939. It was a great blow to the company, but during the Depression the Santa Fe could not afford the luxury of going without a leader for long. The board acted quickly.

Edward Engel was elected as president and chairman of the executive committee within three weeks. Engel was similar to Bledsoe in that he moved up through only the managerial ranks of the railroad, and had never been a crewman, builder or operator. He was born in Ohio in 1874, went to business school in Sandusky, and joined the Santa Fe at the age of 25 as Ripley's stenographer. Known for his quiet efficiency, Engel soon became Ripley's right-hand man; and he became successively president, vice president and executive vice president.

Engel brought his standards of efficiency to the presidency. He was as committed to the technological progress, expansion and improvement of the Santa Fe as Bledsoe had been. Under his direction, the railroad continued its programs to convert locomotive operations to diesel, to streamline and air condition passenger trains,

and to improve train control and operations through innovations in communication.

By 1939, the American economy was showing real signs of recovery. World War II broke out in Europe in September of that year, after which 1000 shopmen were put back on a six-day week. A stock dividend of $2.50 per share was declared that June. Even though agricultural production was slow to catch up to the better conditions, the business climate in the Southwest was much improved.

Santa Fe capital improvement expenditures went up, totaling an optimistic $25 million authorized in 1939 and including the cost of large orders for new cars, both freight and passenger, as well as track rebuilding. The average freight car capacity rose to 43.65 tons. The Santa Fe, in a gesture that must have raised morale, began to build and remodel key buildings. Dearborn Station was refurbished and remodeled. A seven-story office building and station was constructed in Galveston. The Santa Fe, jointly with the Union Pacific and Southern Pacific, remodeled the Los Angeles Union station into something of a showplace.

The station, opened in May 1939, held 16 tracks under umbrella sheds. The architecture and decor of the buildings were inspired by the early Spanish influence prevalent throughout old California. It covered 48 acres. The station proper was connected with the eight loading platforms by almost 500 feet of subway thoroughfare. The project cost $49 million to complete, of which the Santa Fe paid one-third.

The railroads threw a party, attended by what seemed to be most of Los Angeles, to celebrate that station's opening. The Santa Fe draped a train with bunting,

decorative flags and the company trademark, and invited celebrants to climb aboard. Only the most astute could, at the time, have predicted the scale of traffic that would go through that station in a very few years, as men from all over the nation converged upon the West Coast on their way to war.

The Depression was almost over, and the Santa Fe had weathered it well. Plenty of its co-western railroads had found themselves bankrupt, but the Santa Fe's conservative financial policies kept it running, and even turned some small but definite profits in the bargain. The company's assets actually increased during the 1930s, although the increase was slight. This was much more than many American businesses could boast. Investors remained confident in the railroad, which resumed

dividend payments for good in the August of 1939, and whose common stock rallied a bit and was on its way to a moderate recovery in the stock market. And although it was moderate, expansion never ceased.

Decisions to keep expanding and improving, even through the troubled times, to prepare for a better future paid off. As the Depression ended in 1939 and 1940, business and revenues rose. The rains finally returned to the Dust Bowl. Grass was green and cattle were fat again. Bumper wheat crops were harvested. Cattlemen and farmers went back to providing the business which was the mainstay of the Santa Fe. The rate of economic growth in the area had slowed as a result of the Depression, but the population was booming. Happy days, however, were not quite here again. The war which was tearing Europe apart

Though even the Santa Fe's early passenger diesels developed 2000hp apiece, Raton Pass occasioned a helping hand from steam locomotives. *At left, two Santa Fe 2–10–2s assist* El Capitan's *diesel units up the grade in the 1940s. Soon enough, it would be diesels helping diesels.*

3000 special trains, plus contend with the normal load of freight and passengers. On one amazing night, the Santa Fe used 55 trains—22 miles of cars—to move an entire army installation.

The American system of railroads was at the time the cheapest, fastest and most capable system of mass transit in the world. It moved tonnage faster than the army cars and trucks Adolf Hitler favored. Without it, there would have been no point to the massive amounts of planes, tanks, guns, ships, shells, cars, trucks and dynamite manufactured here. These became useful only when moved quickly and efficiently to where they were needed.

There is no question that America's railways, and with them the Santa Fe, played a gigantic part in the United States' war effort and victory. Faced on two fronts by well-prepared, determined and sufficient enemies, the United States had to depend on its network of steel, the locomotives that ran on it, and the carrying power of which it was capable, to move men and material safely and surely where they were needed, when they were needed.

The Santa Fe owned the main line between the crossroads of Chicago and the West Coast. This double-track line was loaded with as much as it could possibly bear and was used to capacity. Passenger traffic rose 88 percent between 1941 and 1942, and ton miles of freight almost doubled. The Santa Fe shared the 82-mile run between San Bernadino and Barstow, and this track alone carried 20 to 30 freight trains every day. Manpower became incredibly short, as the railroads' labor forces either went off to fight or to work in war plants. Hosts of new workers, many of them women, had to be trained.

The Santa Fe's need for motive-power was met by pushing locomotives far beyond the mileage considered normal before the war, buying steam locomotives from the eastern railroads that could spare them, and relying on the enormous capabilities of the diesel locomotives. A diesel locomotive could move 60 freight cars, about 3150 tons, from Kansas City to Los Angeles in 53 hours. The diesel freights covered the territory from Kansas City to Belen and from Winslow to Barstow, while passenger units traveled all the way through from Chicago to Los Angeles.

Some of the steam locomotives regularly went as far as 1788 miles (the Argentine, Kansas to Los Angeles run) or 1590 miles (the Los Angeles to Newton run). To keep up with the service demand on the power plants and other constantly increasing demands, the locomotive shops extended their operations first to two shifts daily and then to three shifts.

It wasn't an easy task, and many people in Washington—notably the Office of Production Management—didn't think the railroads could do it. They advocated the assumption of railway control by the US government. The railroads convinced them not to panic, however, and went on to perform admirably.

All this had to be done with scanty resources, because government freight and government passengers, which made up the major part of the overload, paid only half the regular rates paid by private shippers and civilian pas-

would soon involve the United States, and the railroad industry would be unalterably affected.

World War II

The outbreak of the Second World war posed new and difficult problems for the Santa Fe. It had survived the Great Depression relatively well, but it had not prospered all that much. Many railroads were in trouble and receiving government aid.

World War II brought a vast increase in military traffic. Early on, the railroads—with some help from the US Army and Navy—moved an average of 5000 carloads of war goods per day among 150 war plants, camps and projects all over the nation. They also had to ship 1,500,000 soldiers per six months, a task demanding sengers. So, despite the overload, the Santa Fe suffered huge losses in potential revenue. Edward Engel, president of the Santa Fe from 1939 to 1944, called the military discount rate 'a serious and growing burden.' As the volume of military traffic grew ever-larger, the validity of Engel's statement became painfully obvious, but the war effort necessitated the continuation of the 50 percent rate. The Santa Fe discounted $151,243,773 in freight charges and $38,252,191 in passenger fares between 1942 and 1946, for a revenue loss of $189,495,964. The railroads especially complained of the fact that even raw materials, when moved to federally leased plants, benefited from the discount. The railroad industry eventually took the issue of this last case to the Supreme Court, which ruled in the government's favor. The military discount was abolished on 1 October 1946, but there was, of course, no provision made for any railroad to recapture its wartime losses.

But the railroads remained, above all things, productive. The effects of the war in Europe, which began in 1939, became apparent early to the train industry. Agricultural production, particularly wheat, skyrocketed. Grain transportation had always been a staple of Santa Fe revenue. The company's 1940 Annual Report related that many munitions facilities, aircraft plants and shipyards were established along the Santa Fe rails. Stockholders increased, at one point actually outnumbering employees 53,000 to 41,300. Dividends were paid, totaling $8,635,700, and wages totaled $81 million. Engel announced the largest equipment order in three years, an order valued at $12.5 million, including 2800 freight cars, as well as two more diesel locomotives for passenger trains. And all of this before Pearl Harbor.

After 7 December 1941, both civilian and military traffic increased even more. Santa Fe checked up on some of its branch lines to estimate their value in productivity in the context of the wartime overload. Some didn't measure up, and the company abandoned a total of more than

250 miles of track. More employees were needed to deal with the traffic overload, and the Santa Fe's labor force grew from 47,000 to almost 54,000. Stocks went up, tripling in value from 1941 to 1942.

This particular phenomena happened only once as the US government quickly increased the federal corporate income tax and levied a stiff wartime excess-profits tax. Engel used the Santa Fe's new earnings wisely, decreasing the company's debt with the profits.

Profits were improving, but by this time, they could not be put into expanding or purchasing new equipment—the military had priority on all the necessary materials. Locomotives, cars and tracks were being pushed to their limits and taking quite a beating. In some cases, maintenance simply had to be postponed.

The demands on the Santa Fe were particularly heavy. It served many of the Army, Navy and Marine installations. Stations near Fort Riley, Fort Hood, the San Diego Naval and Marine bases, and Tinker Field were all along the company's normal run. All the troops on their way to the West Coast for transport to duty in the Pacific Theater had to be accommodated and fed, requiring dozens of dining and passenger cars. Many experienced Santa Fe workers went to war themselves—an extra hardship for the railroad. This led the Santa Fe to request permission from the US government to hire Mexican citizens to help out. The government agreed, and when the number of Santa Fe employees swelled to 58,767, 4250 were Mexican, working from Chicago to California. Some 12,000 Santa Fe employees joined the military, which took advantage of their knowledge and experience by placing many of them in railway battalions.

In fact, many men employed by the Santa Fe—firemen, brakemen, mechanics, clerks—simply changed from one uniform into another one, colored olive drab, and went on

Amtrak took over all Santa Fe passenger operations in the 1970s, including the Santa Fe's San Diego-Los Angeles *San Diegan (right)* service. *Below:* A stenciled ad for the *El Capitan* on an ATSF boxcar.

doing the same thing they had done in Chicago, Albuquerque and San Bernadino, except now they were doing it in India, Burma, Italy, France and Africa. The 710th, 713th and 738 Railway Battalions were 'Santa Fe' outfits.

The 731th was even known as the 'Santa Fe Battalion.' It trained at Clovis in 1942, worked the Amarillo-Belen line for awhile, and was sent to Casablanca in 1943. There is no record of them running into Humphrey Bogart, but they did rebuild track, bridges, and establish marshalling yards in Algeria, Tunisia, Italy, France and even Germany, following the Nazis' tail all the way into Karlsruhe in 1945.

A route that carried one of the heaviest burdens was the Los Angeles—San Diego run, an 118-mile 'surfline.' Both cities contained aircraft plants and naval installations, and had close-by army and marine facilities, making them both major cores of military activity. On 5 June 1942, this track carried 4919 people between the two cities, one of the trains running in seven sections. Twenty-four miles of the route were double tracked to maximize capacity. San Diego particularly was almost entirely dependent on the Santa Fe for all railroad services.

The amount of tonnage carried continued to increase, as did operating revenues. However, beginning in 1943, profits actually declined, due to higher wages for labor and the 50 percent military discount. Both passenger and freight rates were lower in 1944 than in 1929. The traffic overload meant that many employees had to work overtime or double-time, and be paid accordingly.

The boxcar shortage was critical. Only 22,700 boxcars could be purchased by all the railroads combined, because materials were being used for military needs. Older cars,

Above: **The gleaming, polished** *Valley Flyer* **gets under way.** *Opposite:* **An ad for the** *El Capitan*, **a non-sleeper service passenger express liner that included most of the other Santa Fe amenities.** *Overleaf:* **The** *San Francisco Chief*, **westbound in Abo Canyon, New Mexico.**

then, were rebuilt instead of being replaced. The Santa Fe bought 26 new cars in 1941, 41 in 1942 and only one in 1943. The federal government pooled freight cars to attempt to meet the needs of the nation, but this pooling hurt rather than helped the Santa Fe because it was a major freight car holder.

Engel, perhaps feeling (despite his admirable performance) too much of the weight of the wartime pressures, retired after 45 years of service in 1944. Fred Gurley took over the offices of president and chairman of the Executive Committee on 1 August 1944. Gurley, then 55, was born in Sedalia, Missouri, in 1889. He had begun his career in railroading at the age of 17 as a clerk at the Chicago, Burlington and Quincy, where he stayed for 33 years. Ralph Budd, CB&Q executive, noticed his talent when by 1925 he had become general superintendent. Budd promoted him to the position of vice president in charge of operations, then just plain vice president. It was with Gurley's help that the *Zephyr* and the diesel were brought to the CB&Q. The young vice president caught the eye of Engel, always a man to spot ability. In 1932, Engel offered him the vice-presidency of the Santa Fe. Gurley accepted.

Engel and Gurley worked as a team. They shared enthusiasm for many railroad innovations, such as streamlined passenger trains, the diesel, and the use of a new technology to solve old railroad problems. Gurley was himself an expert on motive power and operations, making him an excellent choice for leadership of the company during the latter part of World War II.

Gurley left as a priority that the Santa Fe should continue to grow with the Southwest, even during the war. He felt it was important to locate the Santa Fe to attract businesses in urban areas that were still developing, such as Oklahoma City and Long Beach.

Oklahoma City was for the most part served by a local line, the Oklahoma Railway, which did duty as a freight feeder to nearby communities and operated a switching service for the Oklahoma City stockyards and meat-packing plants, as well as various other industries. The Oklahoma Railway put its freight and switching lines up for sale in 1943. The Santa Fe and the Rock Island bought different parts of it for a total of $373,942, the Santa Fe acquiring the 8-mile branch to the stockyards, the Rock Island getting 13 miles within the city limits. The Santa Fe now controlled an important, lucrative switching operation with access to a major industrial area.

Long Beach, meanwhile, grew to a population of 250,000 as the many aircraft plants and harbor operations in the area mushroomed. The Santa Fe had been trying to wrangle a way to reach Long Beach Harbor for 40 years. The war effort now made access absolutely necessary. The company asked the Interstate Commerce Commission for permission to reach it. The ICC recommended that the Santa Fe be given equal access to that afforded the Southern Pacific and Union Pacific. The ICC also initially agreed to let the Santa Fe build two miles of track to the harbor, but this was considered unnecessary when the SP and its local affiliate, Pacific Electric, reached an agreement with the Santa Fe on switching and trackage rights. This, in a time of scarce building materials and profit decline, saved the Santa Fe some much-needed time, energy and money. Thus, Santa Fe Long Beach freight service began on 15 December 1945—and the company was involved in yet another major industrial area.

This was fortunate, because in late 1945 and early 1946, the Santa Fe needed all the business it could get. With the end of the war in August 1945 came a sudden and sharp decline in both passenger and freight business. Profits increased a bit with the end of the military discount and less military business, but now operating revenues fell. Federal taxes were reduced, but the money from the reduction could not cover the high cost of the much-postponed maintenance work that now could be put off no longer.

Moves were made to increase efficiency. Trains were built longer, faster. Passengers per train increased, so there was less wastage of power and fuel. Passenger locomotives were now capable of going more miles in a day than had ever been possible before.

Costs still mounted. Gurley knew some money had to be spent to save money. In 1946 the board authorized capital expenditures of $24.9 million, used for line relocation, grade reduction, new bridges and modern communication devices. Financially, the Santa Fe stayed on its feet.

Extra money was again used to decrease debts. Almost $100 million of loans and obligations were paid. The Santa Fe had always tried to stick to conservative financial policies. This paid off, and the company came out of the war with comparatively little money owed.

After the war, a good deal of the money was spent for modern communications and train dispatching systems, the reasoning being that this would make railroading more efficient. This reasoning proved valid. The Santa Fe began to install CTC, or Centralized Traffic Control, in areas with busy train traffic in 1944. It cost $13,000 per mile, but reduced train-running times by one-third and added to the capacity of single-track lines, sometimes by as much as 80 percent.

Through CTC, a dispatcher in a control room miles from the train could set switches and routes. By looking at a giant control board, the dispatcher could see the trains' locations, marked by small red lights, which changed to reflect the trains' progress. He could then accurately and safely arrange meets, place trains on a siding, and regulate use of second tracks. Despite the initial expenditure required, the Santa Fe expanded the CTC system quickly.

Trackage under CTC control totaled 520 miles by 1946. (Original installation had been 113 miles on the Los Angeles-San Diego run.) The heavily-used San Diego-Los Angeles run, the Belen Cutoff through Abo Canyon in New Mexico, and the main line tracks in Kansas all benefited a great deal from the CTC.

Radio for communications over the rails was another pioneering effort of the Santa Fe. The company first used it 4 June 1944, on a 'Spud Special'—one of the fast freight trains that took potatoes from Bakersfield to Chicago. Until then, train crews had always used a hand and whistle system, often slow and cumbersome. This 'Spud Special' moved down the rails using a two-way radio-telephone set. The Santa Fe equipped trains with a radiophone in the locomotive, one in the caboose, and a matching set in a radio-equipped switcher. With these improvements, trains could be made up and operated by point. Built in 1890, it was the largest cantilever bridge in the United States. However, speed was restricted on it, and the approaches were too sharply curved to be taken very fast. Thus, in 1942, construction of a new bridge began. The project included the deepest pneumatic underwater construction yet attempted in the nation, with piers 121 feet below the river. When completed, the bridge consisted of eight double-track spans of 1500 feet. It opened 8 May 1945, and reduced passenger train schedules by 10 minutes and freight train schedules by 20 minutes.

Two years later, the Santa Fe bridge at Canyon Diablo was similarly replaced. The original bridge was built in 1900, with a gauntlet track added in 1913 to increase capacity. Speed on the bridge, however, was restricted to 10 miles per hour, for safety in the extremely narrow and deep canyon. At a site north of this bridge, workers pumped concrete into the cracks of the limestone canyon walls. Only then could concrete piers for the new bridge be poured. A false-work was used on both sides of the canyon to allow workmen to erect the steel supports, as were huge precautionary safety nets. The 544-foot bridge opened in September 1947. It included a 300-foot hinged arch with 120-foot spans at either side, and had no speed restriction.

Another bottleneck was at the Tehachapi Pass, which the Santa Fe improved jointly with Southern Pacific. However, there was a limit to what could be done on the rugged terrain. There were 18 tunnels on the 28 miles of track, as well as 2.5 percent grades. The rapid agricultural and industrial growth in nearby San Joaquin Valley aggravated the line's growing congestion, and the line was loaded to capacity. CTC was installed on this trackage in 1943, but the speed limit for passenger trains was still 25 miles per hour—20 miles per hour for freight trains (and the 70-car freights still needed 2–10–2 helpers to cover the trackage).

Argentine Yard in Kansas City, another major bottleneck, was in need of improvement but could not be seen to until 1947. The yard handled 4000 cars daily during peak periods, and a quarter consisted of interchanges with the city's 12 other carriers. The old flat yard was replaced, necessitating the move of an entire Kansas town—Turner—to make room for the new 56-track humpyard. Storage tracks, a locomotive terminal and departure yards were included, as well as giant illuminating towers. The yard was outfitted with radio-equipped switches, used for train assemblage, and a pit covered with thick shatterproof glass, used by yardmen to inspect the running gear of the freight cars. When the improvements were finished, Argentine Yard measured four miles long and one-half mile wide—a giant, efficient system at the important crossroad point of Kansas City.

The Santa Fe attended to the health of its system overall, as well as specific problems. Still unable to purchase new cars, even near the end of the war, the company threw its money and energies into track rebuilding and grade improvement. It installed heavier rails—at least 110 pounds—reduced curves and grades, and relocated track to raise speed limits, which were now up to 90 miles per hour on a good portion of the main line. By 1945, there were 1936 miles of double track, 44 miles of triple track, and four miles of quadruple track on the Santa Fe. The Santa Fe had not just 'made it through' the war—it had improved itself.

En route from Los Angeles to Chicago, the *El Capitan (above)* climbs Raton Pass in southern Colorado. Its 'Hi-Level' cars made for better passenger views of the scenery, and provided more storage space below.

radio. Gurley, impressed with the results, created a radio network between Chicago and the West Coast and Chicago and Galveston, including a radio-telephone communications system for yard locomotives and cabooses. By 1946, over 2700 Santa Fe employees worked in communications, and the company adopted a high-frequency multichannel system. The company was now handling the greatest volume of telephone and telegraph messages of any transportation system in the world.

The state-of-the-art communications systems were not the only way Engel and Gurley fought to eliminate traffic 'bottlenecks,' a feat apparently worth millions to them. Bridges, for instance, could be a problem. The Santa Fe's bridge over the Colorado River near Needles was a case in

After the War

The Santa Fe Skyway—Flying Refrigerators

In May, 1946, Gurley announced the formation of Santa Fe Skyway, Inc, as a Delaware corporation and a wholly owned affiliate of the Atchison, Topeka & Santa Fe Company. Santa Fe intended to provide the general area already served by the railroad with air cargo service. With an initial stock value of $100,000, Santa Fe Skyway established a home office in Wichita, Kansas and a headquarters with its parent company at the Railway Exchange in Chicago.

Santa Fe had already had some input into air transportation. The company had joined forces with both Transcontinental Air Transport and Universal Air Linesway back in the July of 1929 to try to provide coordinated air and rail travel between New York and Los Angeles. However, the combined air/rail route, involving several transfers and several days to complete, was not particularly convenient to travelers or profitable to the companies involved. It was scrapped after a year. Santa Fe concentrated on its lucrative and successful passenger train service and Transcontinental Air Transport went on to join forces with two other infant airlines to become TWA.

But this Santa Fe airline was interested in freight. Homer R Lake was appointed as president and George W Lupton, Jr was appointed as vice president and general manager. The Skyway purchased two war surplus Douglas C-47 Skytrains. By the end of August, the planes were tailored to conform to government civil aircraft certification requirements. The work was done at the Grand Central Airport Co in Glendale, California. The Santa Fe also purchased an additional C-47.

The first Santa Fe Skyway air cargo shipment left Los Angeles Municipal Airport at 12:45 pm on 31 July 1946. Captain Steve Doss (Skyway's chief pilot), First Officer E W Harris, Mechanic C S Potter and Ed Wilkes III made up the crew. The plane carried 2600 pounds of strawberries and 400 pounds of swordfish. The swordfish was, not surprisingly, for the Fred Harvey Co. At a stop in Salinas, 450 pounds of melons, peaches and berries, also destined for Harvey Houses and dining cars, were loaded. The plane stopped to refuel in Amarillo, where a fresh crew, consisting of Captain CW Bryant, First Officer RC Neary and Mechanic WF Zadra, came aboard. The flight arrived in Chicago at 6:06 am, Central Standard Time, on Thursday, 1 August 1946—15 hours, 21 minutes after leaving Los Angeles.

Four Douglas C-54 aircraft, capable of carrying more than 10 tons, were now purchased and modified. Expansion continued, with Santa Fe Skyway operating under a temporary and restricted license allowed by the Civil Aeronautics Board pending examination of a petition for a license allowing the skyway to operate as a common carrier. Many such licenses were requested after the war. The Santa Fe's airline built up an impressive record; it

The years following World War II saw a changed Santa Fe. *Below* is a former DC-4 in the service of Santa Fe's promising but government-aborted Santa Fe Skyway. Diesel power such as the Electromotive passenger diesel *at right* truly came into its own after the war.

flew 2,015,000 miles without accident and experienced only five flight cancellations—one due to mechanical problems and the other four due to weather. Santa Fe executives even accompanied the pilots if the plane happened to be headed in a convenient direction.

Besides foodstuffs, the little airline built up a steady business in flying fresh flowers from the West Coast to New York and Chicago. Planes were named for the southwestern Indian tribes, such as the Zuni and the Navajo, to honor the Indians who had helped to build the railroad. Eighteen pilots, 15 mechanics and 10 salesmen were hired. Everything seemed to be going beautifully.

The company was stunned when the Civil Aeronautics Board rejected its petition to operate as a common carrier. The Missouri Pacific's airline subsidiary, Eagle Airlines, was also rejected by the board, which apparently did not approve of airlines controlled by surface carriers.

The Santa Fe had no choice but to withdraw from the air transport field. The Santa Fe Skyway ceased to operate on 15 January 1948. An interesting branch for the Santa Fe—and one that might have helped it during the difficult years that were ahead for the railroad industry—had been nipped in the bud.

Expansion Under Gurley

At the close of World War II, Gurley and his management realized that the Santa Fe had to keep moving forward. Between 1945 and 1955, they worked on expanding the Santa Fe's sources of freight traffic. They purchased specialized cars for specific needs, offered faster and more frequent train service, and encouraged the

Upper left: **Santa Fe club cars catered to passenger comfort on Santa Fe rails in the 1950s, and Santa Fe Skyway freight service *(below)* got off the ground in 1946, only to be grounded permanently in 1948 when the Civil Aeronautics Board refused them a common carrier permit.**

growth industry and new mining operations much as they had encouraged the growth of farms and prairie towns in earlier days. They analyzed traffic, noticing that some freight categories, like petroleum and live cattle, had declined considerably. But there had been a substantial increase in freight traffic for manufactured goods, potash and coal. The operating department offered at least daily service to almost all branches, and deliveries that, if at all possible, were timed to the shippers' needs. The feeling was that these services would increase on-line loadings. On the routes where the Santa Fe faced keen competition, the company strove to reduce running times. The Santa Fe's freight time between Denver and Chicago, for instance, was reduced by eight hours between 1946 and 1954.

The Santa Fe used speed particularly to attract shippers of fresh produce, a business which was growing in the Southwest. The Santa Fe had captured about 43 percent of the California citrus business as early as 1929, and it hung on to this business with the 'Green Fruit Express,' a refrigerated car special. Cars converged at San Bernadino, where they were organized into trains carrying produce exclusively, and sped to Chicago. These cars needed millions of tons of ice, which was provided by icing platforms along the line. There were special trains for transporting the potato crop out of San Joaquin Valley, and, beginning in 1949, a 'Cotton Special' for moving the West Texas cotton crop from the Lubbock area to the Galveston wharves. Shippers could pay an extra $1.25 per hundred pounds to have their cars of produce included in a Bakersfield-Chicago train that operated on a special 62-hour schedule.

Thus agriculture remained a major source of revenue for the Santa Fe, with wheat the single most important commodity. Three-fourths of all the agricultural tonnage came from Kansas, Texas and Oklahoma. By the mid-1950s,

Above: A Santa Fe snow plow. The Baldwin Locomotive Works made powerful freight diesels like this one *(below)* for the Santa Fe, but was fated to follow steam power, Baldwin's 'first love,' into history.

the Santa Fe had developed a diversified business, giving its system the economic strength to cope with the sometimes fickle national economy. Many large systems at the time were dependent on interchange traffic, but not the Santa Fe. Almost two-thirds of its tonnage was loaded and delivered on its own lines. Car movement was very well balanced east to west and north to south. Between Clovis and Belen, for example, movement was almost perfectly balanced. The remaining one-third of the Santa Fe's traffic that was generated from the interchange came, for the most part, from eastern carriers. Almost half of the cars were exchanged at the east-west crossroads of Chicago and Kansas City. Gurley and his administration made their system progressively less dependent on any one source of revenue and on other railroads.

As the southwestern economy blossomed, the Santa Fe blossomed with it, becoming an enormously successful railroad. The populations of California, Texas and Arizona swelled—so did the amount of service they demanded. Traffic volume grew, and the Santa Fe captured over 90 percent of all rail traffic in New Mexico, 45 percent in Kansas, 30 percent in California, and over 20 percent in Oklahoma and Colorado. Almost one-third of all rail freight in the Southwest was moved by the Santa Fe, and almost one-fourth of it originated on Santa Fe rails.

The Santa Fe accommodated the changes and growth in the southwestern economy by purchasing new equipment needed to haul new types of cargoes. New fleets of 'damage free' cars were needed to cover the increasing volume of manufactured goods. LCL traffic, now the province of the truckers, declined, so the Santa Fe found volume replacements, such as potash. The United States Potash Company operation near Carlsbad, New Mexico, had expanded during World War II because European potash was not available. Now potash production grew rapidly, and the Santa Fe built branches to reach the new mines. Carlsbad became, by the mid-1950s, the second largest revenue producing station on the system.

The 'Gurley team' coordinated its operations to come up with an end result of new business, expanded industrial development, and the satisfactory meeting of traffic requirements. After the war, the Santa Fe enhanced its efforts to attract new industries to sites along its lines. Full-time agents in San Francisco, Los Angeles, Galveston and Topeka were added to the industrial department. In 1951, the office of assistant to the president in charge of industrial development was created. This department coordinated the company's industrial development efforts and designated industrial districts or sites at locations advantageous to the Santa Fe. Often the railway would buy land in cities along the line, level existing buildings, build spurs and utility systems, then sell the sites to mercantile and industrial corporations. By 1952 the Santa Fe owned 21 of these sites, each of which included 80 to 160 acres of land available for development. From the end of World War II until 1952, 3100 plants had set up shop along the Santa Fe lines, resulting in $150 million in annual gross revenues for the railroad. The number of industrial sites continued to grow, and thanks to the work of the industrial department they contributed substantially to car loadings.

The advertising department had concentrated mostly on attracting passenger traffic before the war. During the Depression, under Bledsoe, more attention was paid to ads aimed at freight shippers. In 1936, a public relations department was created. This new department assumed responsibility for the Santa Fe Magazine, as well as broadcasting operations and interpreting railway efforts to the public. It also instituted a film bureau, which provided films and travelogues on transportation history, safety and train trips to civic groups and advertising. This left the advertising department free to pursue other areas. It developed a program of institutional advertising, and placed freight-only ads on a large scale nationwide, putting large ads in 950 newspapers, business journals and such magazines as Look and The Saturday Evening Post. The catch-phrase Santa Fe advertisers adopted was 'America's New Railroad.' The advertising department coordinated its efforts aimed at shippers with the work of the industrial department.

The Santa Fe augmented the work it had already done to attract new traffic by building branch lines and purchasing existing feeder lines. For example, in 1947, to improve its access to several large manufacturing operations outside of Chicago, the railroad bought a majority interest in the Illinois Northern Railway, a small, 19-mile railroad that served almost exclusively the International Harvester Company, its owner. Other railroads also purchased parts of the little railway, but the Santa Fe's interest, costing $489,000, protected its part of the traffic. In 1957, the company extended a branch almost 30 miles to service a Kaiser Steel Plant and a Permanente Cement facility at Hesperia, California.

A shining example of this kind of expansion lay in the Santa Fe's costly but productive new branch into Dallas. The Santa Fe had constructed a terminal warehouse complex in the city, but it still could not corner a competitive part of Dallas business. Santa Fe trains had to enter the city via the inconvenient Cleburne-Dallas-Paris branch, which delayed freight movements, forced freight trains to use a lengthy and circuitous route to reach the Chicago-

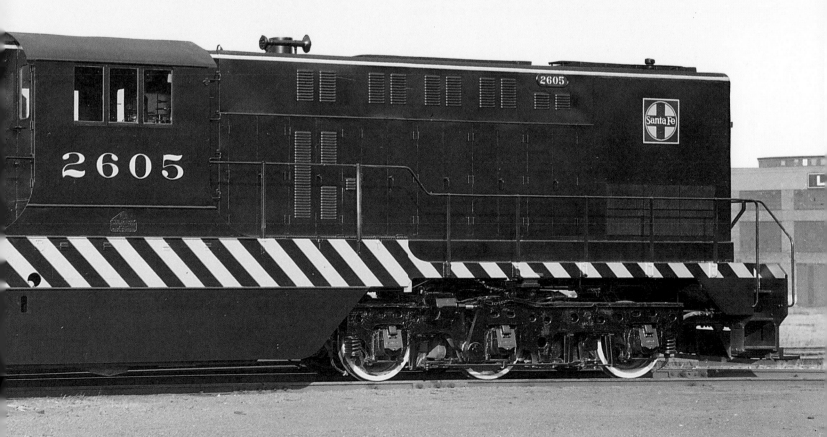

Above: **The road switcher on the right was identical to the circa 1945 passenger loco on the left before the former was rebuilt at the Santa Fe's Cleburne, Texas shops.** *Opposite:* **The *Super Chief* in the 1950s.**

Houston line at Cleburne, and necessitated the moving of Dallas passengers to and from Fort Worth by bus. The Dallas Chamber of Commerce, however, had long wished for the Santa Fe to enter the city from the north and provide a one-carrier direct route to Chicago. In 1951, work began on the surveying of possible routes. In June of 1953, Gurley submitted his proposal to build 38 miles of new track from the main line at Sawyer to a connection with the Cotton Belt at Addison. The Cotton Belt would then be used from Addison to Dallas. This new line would reduce the Santa Fe freight route by 70 miles and give the railroad a 1001-mile route from Dallas to Chicago. The plan was approved after minor changes were made to include the towns of Denton and Richardson. Construction began in late 1954, and the line, the longest main-line construction to be built in 25 years, opened 1 December 1955. The Santa Fe now had access to the area north of Dallas, a booming industrial region. Shipments from Dallas to Chicago took 72 hours less than they had with the old line. It was forecast that during the first five years of the new line's operation it would move 55,000 freight cars. New industrial sites were located on the line, including one of 172 acres in north-

east Dallas. The route cost $7 million, but with it, the Santa Fe had a low gradient, high density track into one of the fastest growing cities in the region. Like so many other projects the Santa Fe had been involved in over the years, the new Dallas line proved a solid investment.

The Santa Fe's astute assessments of investments did not go unnoticed, and the railroad earned a reputation as a well-managed, dependable yet progressive company. In 1948, *Fortune* called the Atchison, Topeka & Santa Fe the 'Nation's Number One Railroad.' It was tightly organized, employee morale was high, and Gurley was considered one of the best executives in the railroad business. Thanks to good planning and strategically located expansion, the Santa Fe earned more from 1946 to 1948 than the New York Central, the Pennsylvania and the Southern Pacific put together. Both dividends and cash reserves grew, and the Santa Fe steadily reduced its debt, as it had always been its policy to do whenever possible. The Santa Fe's only problem in the early post-war years was the enormous increase in both federal and local taxes.

Tax levels were never as high as they had been during the peak period of the war, when total taxes paid by the Santa Fe were two and one half times the total income for 1945. There was a small decline in taxes after the surrender of the Axis powers, but by 1949 the tax bill was high again, equaling $28.47 per share. With the Korean

War came another excess-profits tax as well as higher state and local property taxes. The total tax payment was up to $110 million by 1952. Taxes had become the third largest cost item in the system budget, second only to the payroll, which accounted for 43.4 percent of expenses, and fuel and supplies, which accounted for 15.2 percent of expenses.

Later, other problems emerged. In 1957, operating revenues declined and profits began to slide. Reasons were the increased expenses of dieselization, loss of passenger traffic, the climbing taxes and heavy increase in wages. The board of directors cut capital expenditures in half in 1955 following the complete dieselization of the railroad and were faced with a continuing decline in revenue. The rising labor costs caused a reduction in the total number of employees.

The Santa Fe, however, still stayed at the forefront of American railroads, hailed as one of the rail industry's leaders. Said *The New York Times* in 1955, 'Things hum on the Santa Fe trail.' According to the *Times*: 'Largely because motive power has been completely dieselized, and its yards highly mechanized, and because the management has built one of the greatest communications networks in the world, the performance of the Santa Fe has improved strikingly.' The *Times* also noted the high morale and loyalty of Santa Fe employees and the economic growth

and vitality of the area the railroad served. Such kind words were valued by Gurley and his workers, because they reflected—even at a time when the US rail industry was beginning to deteriorate as a whole and faced much public and political criticism—confidence in the Santa Fe system. And operating revenues and profits did, in general, steadily increase throughout the 1950s and early 1960s. Unlike some of his predecessors, Gurley was able to retire in a year of peace and prosperity—1957, which saw nearly record operating revenues.

Ernest S Marsh succeeded Gurley as president, although his former boss stayed on as chairman of the board and chief executive officer until 1958. Marsh was born in Lynchburg, Virginia in 1903 and moved with his family to Clovis, New Mexico, where in 1918 he joined the Santa Fe. By the age of 39 he was chief clerk in the president's office. Two years later he became assistant to the president, then vice president for finance. In 1958, he took over the responsibilities of chief executive officer from Gurley. In 1967, he took on the role of chairman of the board, a position not utilized between 1959 and 1967.

Marsh was also a graduate of the advanced management program at the Harvard School of Business Administration. He soon found his skills sorely needed. Taxes and wages continued to rise, increasing costs. Losses in passenger business grew. A recession in 1958 didn't help matters. Capital expenditure had to increase to pay for labor-saving plans and devices. Rates were only increased modestly, leaving all railways somewhat between a rock and a hard place. The year 1961 saw the loss of 4000 employees. The Santa Fe also obtained permission to absorb its Texas subsidiaries. This move saved the railroad at least $2 million per year.

Marsh and his executives agreed that action had to be taken to make the line competitive with other railroads, trucking operations and, if possible, pipelines. In 1960, they began a modernization program with an initial budget of $100 million. The system added hundreds of miles of welded rail, 2500 new freight cars and new high-horsepower diesels. It expanded its microwave network. Even larger new equipment orders were placed in 1962, not without the encouragement of the federal government's 7 percent investment tax credit. The 1962 order included 700 'shock-control' insulated boxcars, 50 piggyback flatcars, 200 center-flow covered hoppers and 750 boxcars. In 1965, the order was even bigger and carried a price tag of $115 million, paying for 225 miles of welded rail, 4500 freight cars and 100 diesel locomotives. Triple-deck automobile carriers were included in these orders, which enabled the railroad to take back part of the new car and truck business. In 1966, the capital budget included a $38 million contract, made with the Pullman-Standard works for 2500 'jumbo' covered hoppers. These were used for bulk cargoes like wheat and potash. The period was prosperous, and the operating revenue increased. But the Santa Fe was still far from unburdened financially.

The company had not abandoned its conservative fiscal policies and still reduced its debt whenever it could. But this tremendous outpouring of capital had cost it. In 1960, the Santa Fe owed a total of $199 million, mostly in general mortgage and adjustment bonds and equipment trusts. It had $22.9 million in the voluntary debt retirement fund it had instituted. By 1966, there was $45.5 million in the debt retirement fund—but the debt had jumped to $324 million. The general mortgage debt was only $179 million, with the remaining debt in the form of equipment trusts at $135 million. Equipment trusts had made up only $13 million of the debt in 1960. This demonstrates the Santa Fe management's total commitment to creating the most efficiently managed, well-run and technologically advanced railway in the United States.

Much of the credit for the technological advances of the company goes to President John S Reed, who took over from Marsh in 1967, after Marsh had been appointed chairman of the board. A Yale graduate, Reed was born in Chicago in 1917. He joined the Santa Fe in 1939. He left the railroad temporarily during World War II to serve as a lieutenant commander in the Navy. After rejoining the Santa Fe, he became successively a test department assistant, trainmaster and divisional superintendent at Marceline, Missouri. In 1954, he became assistant to the vice president. Within 10 years he was vice president of the executive department. As president, Reed initiated programs for long-range planning, concentrated on the

need for more highly trained executives, and expected a more efficient utilization of equipment, particularly of the diesel locomotives.

The need for executives highly skilled in 'modern' techniques was one the Santa Fe had recognized as early as 1952. That year, the Santa Fe, in cooperation with the University of Southern California's School of Commerce, began a summer training program for both senior executives and their 'juniors' who stood in line for positions. Expenses for the executives and their families were paid by the railroad. The idea was to provide executives of both the present generation and the generation to come with advanced business skills. The Santa Fe also began to seek out prospective employees with the technical skills to operate the data processing center in Topeka, and the computerized inventory control in purchasing, for the executive and operating departments.

Modernization under Reed

Equipment acquisition was accelerated even more under Reed, as was line rebuilding. One of the Santa Fe's most important sources of new revenue came from the transport of truck trailers on flatcars (called TOFC or 'piggybacks') and metal containers on flatcars. In 1952, the company began experimenting with trailers on flatcars. 'Dry Ice' trailers were used several times to transport semi-perishable projects. The program proved so successful that by 1954 the Santa Fe provided piggyback service from Chicago to both the West Coast and the Gulf of Mexico.

Flatcars carrying two trailers each became a common sight along the Santa Fe lines. Soon trains made up of only piggyback cars became a necessity. Many trailers could be provided by the truck subsidiary the Santa Fe had already established, but most of the trailers used were still rail-industry-owned. As the piggybacking business

Opposite: **Pulling a train across the Illinois River, these modern road switchers underscore the Santa Fe's increased freight service in this, its post-passenger era. 'Fuel-Foiler' piggyback container trains *(above and below)* exemplify the Santa Fe's intermodal freight service.**

grew, the Santa Fe built depressed-deck flatcars 88 feet in length. These cars lowered their centers of gravity, enabling them to carry long trailers with more stability. Between 1968 and 1972, TOFC business grew from 113,523 trailers to 156,262 trailers. During those same four years, the number of sealed metal containers transported by flatcar grew from 1626 to 22,749. Much of this increase could be credited to Reed. The containers were usually on their way to shipment overseas, especially to Japan and other Asian countries. Reed and his executives paid a special visit to the Orient, and business from that sector improved. Much of the capital outlay was spent on equipment necessary to the expansion of the trailer and container business, such as loading platforms and cranes, but the growth in traffic more than justified the expenditures.

The expensive line-rebuilding projects also began to generate returns. In 1955, the Santa Fe began a major program to cut its track maintenance expenses. A key part of this program was the installation of welded rail. At first, short lengths of rail on the line were welded with machinery carried on flatcars. Later, when the value of welded rail in reducing maintenance costs had proved indispensable, fixed facilities were established to weld ribbons of rail which were then moved to the sites where they were needed on trains of flatcars. In 1960, grade-reduction efforts were continued. A new 44-mile line was constructed west from Williams, Arizona to Crookton. This route was integrated into the main line and cost $20 million. It both eliminated clearance restrictions and established a faster (60-mile-per-hour) speed limit for trains. In order to reach the Phoenix branch line, part of the old main line between Williams and Ash Fork remained operative. This line, which had long been a problem as a bottleneck, got a $3.5 million renovation including 38

miles of new track cutting through Skull Valley. This reduced the distance to Phoenix by 14 miles and decreased the grades and curvature that the locomotives had to manage. Similar changes were made in 1972 at the Cajon Pass. Although grades could not be reduced at the pass, curves were cut down and the running time was reduced by seven minutes.

The problems involved in moving freight through yards were also addressed through technical innovations, as was the need for greater, more efficient utilization of motive power. In 1970, the Santa Fe opened its new 48-track computerized yard, which could sort 8000 cars per day, in Kansas City. Secretary of Transportation John Thorpe attended the opening. At the new yard, electromagnetic identification scanners guided the cars onto their proper tracks. With this system, classification time was reduced by 50 percent. In the same year the Santa Fe established a centralized control bureau at its headquarters in Chicago. This bureau directed and coordinated the assignment of diesel units and cabooses. In this way, the Santa Fe hoped, its $300 million fleet of diesels could be utilized with the very maximum of efficiency. The centralized system included a large display board with magnetic markers that maintained a continuous record of the locations and availability of all locomotives. Thus the bureau could provide data on locomotive and caboose requirements for the entire operating system to the operating department.

The Santa Fe once again emphasized speed in its operations, something it had not done since the days of the great *Super Chief*. In 1968, Reed announced a new all-TOFC and container freight train, the *Super C*, which

At right: **A Santa Fe triple header freight barrels through the green countryside.** *Below:* **As modern as this Santa Fe General Electric 2800 hp road switcher is, since this photo was taken, even more advanced and efficient locomotives have come to the fore.**

ran a 34 and one-half hour schedule between Chicago and Los Angeles. This train made its first appearance on January 17. It was one of the world's fastest freight trains and moved at an average speed of 63.7 miles per hour. The Santa Fe also used the train in cooperation with one moving over the Penn-Central from the East Coast, providing a 54-hour, 20-minute route from New York to Los Angeles. Shippers paid a premium of $1400 per trailer, but apparently many felt it was well worth it. The *Super C* became a well-utilized Santa Fe service.

Many critics, however, said of the *Super C* that a railroad should sell bulk, not speed. But the Santa Fe did not rely on flashy, super-fast trains at the expense of the bulk-cargo aspect of the business. The railway had great potential as a conveyor of heavy bulk cargoes at low rates. For instance, it used the new idea of a unit train in two major ways. A unit train was a semi-permanently coupled body of freight cars and locomotives that hauled a single commodity. Coal was one commodity with which it was used. The Santa Fe's coal-hauling traffic had declined with the advent of the diesel locomotive. Extensive coal fields served by the Santa Fe near Raton were kept operating only by the demands of World War II. But in 1955, Kaiser Steel Company purchased 202,835 acres of coal land near Raton as a source of fuel for its Fontana, California plant. In 1964, after exploring its holdings, Kaiser was ready to open a large mine at York Canyon in the Sangre de Cristo Mountains. The Santa Fe built a 37.5 mile heavy-duty branch to the mine and created a unit-train for coal to transport the fuel to California. Kaiser needed 700,000 tons of coal per year, so the Santa Fe bought 101 coal cars that carried 100 tons each, as well as 11 diesel units to provide power. This unit train could take 8400 tons of coal to the plant every four days. The branch cost $4 million to construct, while the unit train cost $2 million. The train went into operation on 28 September 1966. Its first run was a 2164-mile round trip, which represented the longest distance covered by a unit train on a single railroad.

The Santa Fe created another important unit train three years later. The Duval Corporation was at work on plans to develop a sulphur mine at Rustler Springs, Texas, close to the Coleman Cutoff. Duval needed transport for the sulphur to Galveston, from which point it could be shipped by water. Sulphur is difficult to move by rail, but engineers at both the Santa Fe and the Duval Corporation came up with an ingenious plan to transport the substance in a molten state. The sulphur was heated to 290 degrees and fed into large tank cars. It was then shipped to Galveston. By the time it got there, there was still enough heat in the cars to allow the shipment to be unloaded easily. A new 30-mile branch was built to the plant, and three unit trains of 66 cars each were purchased for the 930-mile run to Galveston. The trains traveled from the mine to Galveston and back in continuous movement. Once again, the Santa Fe had used new technology and an investment of capital to attract new and profitable business.

For the Santa Fe, then, the period after the Korean War was marked by the acquisition of new lines and the construction of new branches. It did not buy up lines indiscriminately, however, but limited its purchases and projects to lines that could feed additional cars into the system or strengthen its competitive position. One ex-

Diversity of freight shipments helps the Santa Fe to stay on top. *Above:* A five-header coal train rounds a desert curve. *At right:* The five EMD 3600hp road switchers shown here haul a piggyback train loaded with truck trailers. These engines are 'cowl units'—their broad fronts function as weather proofing and as cosmetic devices.

ample of this was the company's acquisition of the Toledo, Peoria and Western Railroad, which operated 239 miles of track from Lomax, Illinois—a stop also served by the Santa Fe—through Peoria to Effner, Indiana—a stop also served by the Pennsylvania Railroad. This line served as a bridge to bypass the congested traffic in Chicago. It hauled 120,000 cars per year and switched 18,000 more.

It was a line with a troubled history. During the 1940s, it experienced violent conflicts between its owners and employees—so much so that the federal government had to step in and run the line from 1942 to 1945. Yet it was an up-to-date, well-constructed road with 41 miles of welded rail and 7500 acres of industrial land along its route. It had also been dieselized. In 1955, the Santa Fe made its first offer to purchase the TP&W. It proposed to buy 82 percent of the common stock at $135 per share. When the Pennsylvania asked to be included in the purchase, the management agreed to a 50-50 division of the stock. The ICC agreed to the arrangement in 1957, although the final transfer of stock did not take place until 1960. Thus the Santa Fe had, at a cost of $6.1 million, acquired half-interest in a technologically modern line which became an important transcontinental link and Chicago bypass.

In 1962, the Santa Fe purchased the Oklahoma City-Ada-Atoka Railway, a 105-mile line which ran from Oklahoma City through Ada to Tupelo, Oklahoma. It had been part of the so-called 'Muskogee lines,' which included the Kansas, Oklahoma and Gulf and the Midland Valley lines. When a subsidiary of the Missouri Pacific Railway, the Texas and Pacific Railway, bought these lines, the Santa Fe offered to buy the OC-A-A for $1 million. This gave the Santa Fe access to Tinker Air Force

Base and allowed it to abandon some less useful branches, continuing its program of track reduction in central and northern Oklahoma.

New Questions, New Answers

After 1960, the question of mergers became important to the railroad industry. The ICC did its best to protect the industry from mergers that would be destructive to competition, such as the Southern Pacific's attempt to obtain a controlling interest of Santa Fe stock, but the word 'merger' had become synonymous with financial health for railroads. In the East and South of the United States, almost every major carrier was involved in one way or another with mergers or merger plans. In the midwest, the 'Granger' roads were financially troubled, and mergers in that area began to develop. The Norfolk and Western took over the Wabash, while the Chicago and Northwestern acquired the Minneapolis and St Louis and the Chicago Great Western. No one had yet got hold of the Chicago, Rock Island and Pacific, however. This road touched almost every major city between Canada and the Gulf of Mexico and became much sought-after, with interested parties including, besides the Santa Fe, the Union Pacific, the Southern Pacific and the Chicago and Northwestern. The UP wanted to buy all of the Rock Island north of Kansas City and sell what was left to the SP. The CNW wanted to buy the Rock Island and sell everything south of Kansas City except the line to Tucumari (to the Santa Fe), as well as give the Santa Fe trackage rights to St Louis. Every railroad in the region filed an interested party petition. The ICC began what was probably the most complex series of hearings in its history, taking seven years.

The process was further complicated by the financial collapse of the Penn-Central. As a result of this, some roads became stronger, others weaker. The position of the CNW changed; it was now separated from what had been its holding company. The ICC examiner finally issued a report which favored the plan of the Chicago and Northwestern and the Santa Fe. It also urged that several massive mergers take place in the West. It was the examiner's plan to create four 'super-railroads.' The plan included the acquisition by the Santa Fe of not only part of the Rock Island, but also the Missouri Pacific, the Western Pacific and the Denver, Rio Grande and Western.

While the ICC considered this proposal, the Santa Fe explored the financial territory in an attempt to find its own merger partners. Between 1963 and 1965, it talked to both the Missouri Pacific Railroad and the Frisco about possible mergers. The Mississippi River Corporation, which controlled the MP, was very enthusiastic, but the Santa Fe worried over the tangled state of the MP's securities, and the talks came to nought. The Frisco was a railroad with which the Santa Fe had done business before, but the price on it was higher than the Santa Fe was willing to pay. The MP urged a resumption of its talks with the Santa Fe, but the Santa Fe decided to put a stop to the merger negotiations.

The Santa Fe had decided to try a different tack altogether. It had long concentrated on being a diversified corporation as well as a great railway, and boasted activities in trucking, oil, real estate and lumber. With railroad profits either standing still or on the decline in the United States, the board and management decided to create a new holding company of which the railroad would be only one part. In this way, the company could escape restrictions placed on the railway and possibly receive tax advantages and better profits. Thus, in the November of 1967, Santa Fe Industries was formed.

Santa Fe Today

An Open Future

The Santa Fe Southern Pacific Corporation was formed in 1983 as the parent company of Santa Fe Industries, Inc and its affiliates, and Southern Pacific Company and its affiliates. The Southern Pacific Company, which included 13,000 route miles as well as a trucking operation, was held in trust until the ICC made a decision on the proposed merger of the two companies. The initial request by the Santa Fe was denied, as was, on 30 June 1987, the Santa Fe's appeal. The ICC both times rejected the merger on the grounds that it would reduce competition in the West. Thus, within two years, many of the Santa Fe's operations must be sold off.

Among the operations which were acquired when the parent company was formed, and which will now probably have to be sold off, are three pipelines—the Black Mesa, Chaparal and Gulf Central—the Santa Fe Pacific Timber Co; Bankers Leasing and Financial Corporation; and at least one of the century-old railroads—the Southern Pacific Transportation Co, or the Atchison, Topeka and Santa Fe Railway Co. Executives have hinted that the corporation will probably sell the San Francisco-based Southern Pacific, keeping the Santa Fe. Other railroad companies have already expressed interest in the Southern Pacific.

Since the future is not certain for the company, the operations under its ownership at the time of writing are detailed here. The Santa Fe itself is financially healthy, and it is safe to say it will be around in some form or another for some time to come.

The Santa Fe Southern Pacific Corporation's diversified operations are centered in four major business areas: transportation, natural resources, real estate and services and construction.

Transportation: Railroads and Pipelines

Rail, pipeline and truck systems provide the company with a broad base in transportation. The Atchison, Topeka & Santa Fe Railway, with approximately 11,650 route miles, stretches from the Gulf of Mexico at Houston and Galveston, and through the Southwest to the Pacific Coast ports of San Francisco, Los Angeles and San Diego. The Southern Pacific Transportation Company reaches west from St Louis, Kansas City, Memphis and New Orleans across the southwestern United States and up the West Coast as far as Portland Oregon. SPTCo's trucking company has authority to operate in 48 states, but primary operations involve transporting automobiles in the West. The company's four pipeline systems, if combined, would

Above: **Engineers of Southern Pacific (at photo left) and Santa Fe locomotives shake hands, symbolizing the readiness of both railroads to merge.** *At right:* **East- and westbound hotshot freights pass one another at Tehachapi Loop, on the Santa Fe's Mojave Subdivision.**

represent the third longest products pipeline operation in the United States, and the second largest system in terms of the volume of products handled. These systems handle refined petroleum products to customers in six Western states, natural gas liquids across Texas to the Houston area, anhydrous ammonia fertilizer from Louisiana to the Corn Belt states, and coal slurry from Arizona to a power plant in Nevada.

Declines in the nation's basic industries and agricultural economies, which traditionally have been the railroad industry's primary sources of revenue, have coupled with growing competition from the deregulated trucking industry to put pressure on both volume and prices for the railroads. During 1986, management completed a major plan designed to restructure the railroad to enable it to

cope with these changes and compete more successfully. This plan, which will take several years to complete, involves the proposed sale or abandonment of approximately 3100 miles of track, including line segments and yards, and disposition of about 7900 freight cars and 200 locomotives. In addition, it is anticipated that approximately 4100 employees will be laid off. This program was announced in November, and by year-end more than 800 employees had already been laid off. Employment on the Santa Fe Railway, which was 34,950 in 1980, was down to 22,400 at the close of 1986. This restructuring program should lead to important cost reductions beginning in 1987, and, the railroad believes, an increasingly efficient operation in the future.

Operating income in 1986 was up from 1985. This was a good result, considering that freight car-loadings and revenue ton miles were down 3 percent, and average revenue per car was down 4 percent from the previous year. This result was achieved primarily through a tight cost-control program, including an 8 percent reduction in employment, and a 44 percent reduction in fuel expense.

The Santa Fe continues to resist efforts being made by some groups to re-regulate the railroads. The freedoms in pricing, equipment utilization and contracting of services gained under deregulation are extremely important to the company as it endeavors to compete effectively with other modes of transportation which are not only deregulated, but subsidized by the government to the extent that they

do not pay adequate user charges for the rights of way provided them.

The Santa Fe also enjoyed a 14 percent increase in grain shipments in 1986 to 149,000 cars, despite the fact that grain exports were down during the year. Most of the increase came from government grain-relocation movements, primarily wheat and milo, and special marketing programs designed to capture business from trucks. Coal shipments of 263,000 carloads for the year were down six percent, reflecting decreased demand by electrical generating stations.

The Santa Fe made an agreement in 1985 with CP Rail and The Soo Line which was designed to provide improved service between Canada and the United States, which proved very successful, generating about $17 million in gross revenues during 1986.

The Santa Fe physical plant and fleet are still maintained in excellent condition. In 1986, the company laid 251 miles of new and 78 miles of reconditioned welded rail, replaced 1.8 million ties and resurfaced about 6000 miles of track. It also remanufactured 120 diesel locomotive units in its own shops, and purchased 150 multi-level auto racks for installation on flatcars.

During 1987 fixed plant improvements included installation of 235 miles of new and 63 miles of reconditioned welded rail, insertion of 1.5 million ties and resurfacing

Above opposite: **Ten-Pack Fuel-Foiler cars (see page 95) are being prepared for their container loads.** *Opposite:* **SF and SP trains cross paths at Tehachapi Loop.** *Above:* **Santa Fe diesel servicing at Barstow.** *Overleaf:* **SF and SP road switchers, headed in the same direction.**

5400 miles of track. The remanufacturing of 64 diesel locomotive units in Santa Fe shops and the purchase of an additional 90 multi-level auto racks were also planned.

Recently, the Santa Fe and operating unions reached an agreement for inauguration of an experimental 'Quality Service Network.' These new trains operate with reduced crews over longer crew districts than regular trains, and are designed to attract traffic in specified markets where trucks are dominant. It also initiated programs to run freight trains greater distances without changing crews at several points along the railroad.

The stock of Southern Pacific Transportation Company is being held in a voting trust pending resolution of the proposal to merge it and Santa Fe Railway. Under the terms of that voting trust, SPT operates independently.

Southern Pacific's railroads embarked on a restructuring designed to make the company more productive and efficient. In 1986, SPT directors approved write-offs of $601 million to align its assets more closely with the market. The write-offs covered reduction of about 3100 miles of track, disposal of 9800 unneeded freight cars and 400 locomotives, and the laying off or relocation of about

3800 employees. Some of these reductions have already been accomplished; others were planned to take place over several years.

Railroad employment was trimmed eight percent to 26,100 in 1986, and payroll costs were reduced in excess of $80 million. This was accomplished primarily through a voluntary program, in which union employees are offered cash for their seniority rights, and an early retirement program offered to non-union personnel.

International shipments are being speeded by the November, 1986 opening of the $80 million Intermodal Container Transfer Facility in Southern California. A joint project of the Ports of Los Angeles and Long Beach, and served exclusively by SPT, this is the nation's largest intermodal yard devoted to international traffic. Equipped with the latest computer technology, the 150-acre yard can handle 360,000 containers a year.

Intermodal traffic also is increasing because of expedited trains on several important traffic corridors. SPT's *Track Star* trains feature restricted train lengths and reduced crew sizes and compete vigorously to attract traffic from trucks. SPT won the prestigious Golden Freight Car award in 1986 for its marketing of *Track Star* service.

In November 1986 SPT also introduced its Liberator software program, which links a customer's personal computer directly to SPT's mainframe computer. Customers can locate shipments, determine intermodal rates, and generate shipment related instructions from their offices at their convenience. Free to SPT shippers, Liberator is the most advanced system of its kind in the rail industry.

SPT has maintained its commitment to improving facilities with a $374 million capital program in 1986 for roadway, yards and equipment; another $333 million was planned for 1987.

A total of 532 track-miles of welded rail was laid in 1986, of which 220 miles were new; about 2 million ties were replaced, and 3860 miles of track were resurfaced. Another 53,000 rail joints were eliminated by on-track welding to provide smoother and more easily maintained track.

SPT reconstructed and expanded automotive handling facilities at Phoenix, Arizona, and at Marne, near Los Angeles. In 1987, SPT began to rehabilitate an auto handling facility at Valla, near Los Angeles, and to expand intermodal facilities at Dallas.

Equipment acquisitions in 1986 included 300 centerbeam flatcars (which can carry 100-ton loads of lumber), 100 container flatcars, 43 plain flatcars, 32 double-stack container flatcars (each able to carry 10 containers), and 150 fully enclosed bi-level cars to transport new autos or trucks. Thirty-two locomotives were rebuilt in SPT shops. Acquisition of 100 more multi-level cars for auto transport, 40 more double-stack cars and 100 more container flatcars was planned for 1987.

Southern Pacific posted one of the best safety records in its 124-year history in 1986, leading the nation's major railroads. Other programs lowering costs and improving productivity and service include the reduced-crew *Track Star* trains. In 1986, 377 miles of line were sold or leased to short-line operators, and abandonment of 67 miles of branch lines was authorized by the Interstate Commerce Commission.

Opposite: **A Santa Fe quadruple header piggyback train crosses the Colorado River near Needles, California.** *Above:* **A westbound mixed freight descends the rugged and arid Cajon Pass grade.**

SPT's trucking group experienced productivity improvements in the auto transport and intermodal divisions. 1987 plans were to add 110 auto transport units to the fleet, including intermodal trailers for handling new automobiles, utilizing railroad line-haul from assembly plants and local delivery over highways.

Santa Fe's 3010-mile refined petroleum products pipeline system, Santa Fe Pacific Pipelines, Inc, is the largest in the Western United States, serving Oregon, California, Nevada, Arizona, Texas and New Mexico. It handles gasoline, diesel, jet fuel and other products for commercial and military customers in those states.

During 1986, major projects for the system included construction of a new 12-inch pipeline from Concord to Brentwood, California; replacement of 11 miles of six-inch line between Roseville and Reno, Nevada, and installation of new pumps on the Concord-Sacramento line. In 1987 initiation of the second phase expansion of the Northern California system by construction of a new 23-mile, 12-inch pipeline between Sacramento and Roseville, California was begun.

In addition, Santa Fe's 806-mile Chaparal Pipeline delivers natural gas liquids from Eastern New Mexico and West Texas to fractionation facilities near Houston.

Anhydrous ammonia fertilizer moves through the 1943-mile Gulf Central Pipeline from Gulf Coast manufacturing plants to customers throughout the Midwest. Although large crop reductions are expected to cut fertilizer demand in the future, the Santa Fe is optimistic and has constructed a new lateral in Missouri that should add in excess of 75,000 tons of volume annually. Black Mesa Pipeline, the world's largest operating coal slurry pipeline, delivers coal slurry from northeastern Arizona to a power plant in southern Nevada. Black Mesa produced record earnings in 1986 while transporting 4.8 million tons of coal.

Real Estate: Developing Our Nation

Real estate affiliates pursue a program of developing, marketing and managing properties in 16 states in the West, Southwest and Midwest. Maximum value from these real estate assets is derived through a program of developing properties for the company's own account and in joint venture for industrial, commercial and residential uses.

Santa Fe Pacific Realty Corporation carries out a program of development, leasing, sales and property management designed to create maximum value from a large and diverse real estate portfolio. This portfolio includes the company's own holdings, as well as properties that became surplus to the needs of Santa Fe Southern Pacific Corporation's other subsidiaries.

During 1986, SFSPC made significant acquisitions of properties. These included approximately two million square feet of fully-leased structures, including research and development buildings, warehouses, small office buildings, and neighborhood shopping centers.

The company expects to sustain its current level of building two to 2.5 million square feet of new buildings each year in major markets. These will include industrial, light-manufacturing, research and development, low-rise office and warehouse buildings. Santa Fe Pacific Realty manages more than 10 million square feet of properties under its ownership.

The majority of its effort has been directed at Southern California, but in 1986, it was also active in Northern California and expanded significantly in the Phoenix area, where it completed two new projects and acquired others.

In the San Francisco Bay area, the company continues to progress through regulatory bodies plans for its 208-acre Mission Bay project, located about one mile from the city's financial district, plus projects planned for holdings in the East Bay. It completed the largest office lease in the history of Santa Clara County, California, when McDonnell Douglas leased a major portion of its 440,000-square-foot complex in San Jose (now called the McDonnell Douglas Center) as the regional headquarters for its information systems group.

At top, above: **The lead locomotives of this Santa Fe freight display the SFSP merger color scheme.** *Above:* **Long freights under dramatic Western skies—that's the Santa Fe!** *Right:* **This eastbound intermodal freight is leaving Caliente Horseshoe Curve in the far background.**

The planned expansion of the Pacific Design Center in West Hollywood, California, continues too. This expansion will add 450,000 square feet to this fully leased project.

In San Diego, ground was broken for a new 335-room Embassy Suites hotel on its 20-acre waterfront parcel. Santa Fe is the managing partner and half-owner in this project together with the Holiday Corporation. Construc-

Above: **Hopper cars full, this Santa Fe Southern Pacific freight makes a run near Buenos, Texas. Both the SF and the SP are vital to—and depend upon—freight movements in the abundant West and Southwest.**

tion of office and commercial components in San Diego is anticipated in the future.

Santa Fe is also in the process of determining the best course of action for disposing of its 158,000 acres of farmland in California's San Joaquin Valley, half of which must be sold by 1994 under terms of a federal water reclamation law. It sold its equity interest in a large geothermal energy project in southern California, but retains a royalty interest in other properties with geothermal potential.

Natural Resources: Fuel, Forest and Precious Minerals

Natural resources activities at the Santa Fe include petroleum and hard minerals exploration, development, production and marketing, as well as timber operations. Petroleum operations involve onshore oil and gas explora-

several decades. The company has approximately nine million acres of mineral rights in the Southwest, and an active mineral exploration program is under way.

Approximately 520,000 acres of timberland in Northern California are also owned and managed. Douglas fir, true fir, sugar pine and ponderosa pine are produced on these properties.

A continuing worldwide surplus of crude oil and a North American surplus of natural gas has forced prices for these commodities into a steep decline.

It is Santa Fe Energy's assumption that the recent changes in the industry are not temporary, but represent a long-term trend in which prices will increase slowly. This reordering of the industry is expected to produce a healthy business environment toward the end of the decade. As a result, steps were taken to prepare Santa Fe Energy and its affiliates to compete in this new environment, based on Santa Fe Southern Pacific's commitment to oil and gas as a core business.

By mid-1987, SFSP had reduced its work force by about 25 percent, compared to late 1985. In addition, it made significant cuts in other general and administrative expenses and reorganized as a leaner, more streamlined operation. For example, a 50 percent reduction was made in exploration expenditures from 1985 to 1986. Operating expenses were cut $76.3 million—or 32 percent.

Santa Fe Energy has maintained its position as one of the largest independent oil and gas producers in the nation, producing from fields in 14 states, the Gulf of Mexico and offshore California. It actively manages most of its onshore production, directly operating wells representing 68 percent of its total production. Through a combination of exploration, development, and acquisition, it more than replaced its 1986 production with new reserve additions.

Santa Fe Energy Partners LP, a publicly traded limited partnership, was formed from certain assets of Santa Fe Energy Company, that were assigned to the partnership in early 1986. Approximately 20 percent of the company's oil reserves and 90 percent of gas reserves were included in the partnership. Approximately 20 percent of the units in that partnership were owned by the public at the end of 1986, with the company retaining the balance. An affiliate of Santa Fe Energy Company acts as the managing general partner.

Santa Fe's exploration activity includes a program involving over 9 million acres of oil and gas rights on lands owned by the company or its affiliates. Much of this acreage is outside proven oil and gas provinces. Its frontier potential is being explored through agreements with industry partners.

A continuing exploration program is essential for an oil and gas company to remain successful over the long term, since new reserves must constantly be added to replace those depleted through production. Santa Fe Energy is active in exploration efforts.

Recently, the company was particularly successful in offshore exploration efforts, registering four discoveries in 1986. Its interests in these discoveries ranged from 16 to 29 percent. Plans to continue an active offshore exploration program were continued in 1987. The company retains interests in over 75 'blocks' in the Gulf of Mexico and offshore California totaling over 88,000 net acres.

tion and development, and participation in offshore joint ventures. Approximately 20 percent of the company's oil reserves and 90 percent of its gas reserves were placed in a publicly-traded limited partnership. Approximately 20 percent of the total units in that partnership were owned by the public at the end of 1986, with the company retaining the balance.

Ongoing income is derived from coal royalties and production. Shipments from the company's first coal mine began in 1984, and are expected to continue for

Onshore, testing began on a potentially important oil discovery in the Lower Tuscaloosa tract in Mississippi, where Santa Fe is the operator. The Santa Fe holds a 40 percent interest in this discovery, and hopes to start production during 1987. In Texas, it continues to expand on an earlier gas discovery in the Britt Ranch Field, operating and owning a 40 percent interest in the six wells drilled to date.The company continues to explore over 4200 net acres in the area.

In Oklahoma, exploitation of the company's Red Fork and Springer playas in the Anadarko Basin yielded substantial gas reserves. In southeast New Mexico, Santa Fe participated in a gas discovery near the prolific Indian Draw field. Future wells in the field are planned, with Santa Fe interests ranging from 20 percent to 80 percent.

In the international arena, Santa Fe Energy's holdings consist of over 1.4 million net acres located in Tunisia, Indonesia and Columbia. Exploratory drilling was conducted on three concessions in 1987, where Santa Fe interests ranged from 17.5 percent to 50 percent.

The company also completed construction of a new California crude oil terminal in 1986. This new terminal has been connected to two pipelines, and includes facilities for truck loading and unloading. This terminal facility provides the ability to offer crude oil to a wider variety of potential purchasers, especially those on the West Coast.

Demand for coal has fallen sharply in the Southwest, as natural gas and oil have become cheaper for generating electrical power. Santa Fe Pacific Minerals responded by reducing coal production to fit demand and by practicing strict cost control throughout the business. The company established itself as a substantial Western coal producer

with the opening in 1984 of the Lee Ranch Mine. It currently owns more than 9 million acres of mineral rights and nearly 763 million tons of coal reserves in New Mexico, including the Lee Ranch Mine. Of this amount, 490 million tons are under lease.

During its second full year in operation, the mine produced 1.5 million tons of coal, down 29 percent from the 2.2 million tons produced in 1985.

Both of the mine's power plant customers, which have capacity to generate power for sale to other utilities, experienced a rapid drop in demand for power generated by coal after oil and natural gas prices fell precipitously in early 1986. As a result, both plants reduced their coal requirements.

Because of industry problems, no new power plants are expected to come on line for the rest of the decade in the Southwest. The Santa Fe is, therefore, competing for business offered by existing power plants as present contracts come up for renewal. But the company has continued to search for attractive new coal properties throughout the United States. As part of the national effort, Santa Fe established an exploration office in 1985 in Pittsburgh, Pennsylvania to assess coal opportunities in the East.

They have an active inventory of exploration projects in progress. Most of these projects involve exploration to discover new ore deposits that may ultimately be developed into commercial mining operations. Gold and silver exploration work is under way primarily in Nevada and Montana. It is also exploring for specialized industrial minerals, such as calcium carbonate, silica, talc, specialty clays, kaolin and construction aggregates.

In 1986, Santa Fe sold Kirby Forest Industries, which owns timberlands in Texas and Louisiana, and manufac-

turing complexes, for $315 million; it still maintains a significant role in the timber business through Santa Fe Pacific Timber Company's ownership of 520,000 acres in northern California.

The company's goal is to maintain the timber properties in a managed state that will assure continuing growth, along with the ability to increase harvests. One tool which helps to achieve that goal is a sophisticated computerized inventory which reflects volume and rate of growth of each species by geographic location. Harvesting plans based on this inventory are developed five years in advance, and are designed to meet the stringent requirements of the California Department of Forestry relating to environmental concerns and reforestation.

Santa Fe Pacific Timber owns about five percent of the forest acreage in the area of Northern California, but produces about six percent of the timber volume. The entire operation is conducted by a relatively small staff of 63 permanent employees and 33 seasonal employees. All harvesting is supervised closely, but the logging, hauling and reforestation are done on a contract basis rather than with a large staff, enhancing flexibility.

The majority of logs are marketed in Northern California and Oregon, but this varies. For example, in 1985 about seven percent of the harvest was marketed to Japan and the People's Republic of China.

Due to narrowed margins in the lumber business, many Santa Fe mills have been forced to specialize in order to survive. This specialization means that each has unique requirements with regard to species and size of log. Santa Fe's strategy has been to maintain close contact with each mill to determine its requirements. Bids may be made on a stumpage basis, where the customer buys the standing

SFSP's diversification program includes such projects as Santa Fe Energy Partners, LP's onshore (left opposite) and offshore (right opposite) oil exploration programs, and Santa Fe Southern Pacific construction (at left and at top) and engineering (above) projects.

timber and all species marked to be sold, constructs any necessary roads and performs the harvesting and hauling of the timber to the mills. As an alternative, customers can elect to purchase only the desired species, and Santa Fe will deliver those logs to the mill.

The majority of Santa Fe Pacific Timber properties are mountainous in nature, and do not lend themselves to the plantation approach to reforestation practiced in other geographic areas. Each parcel is treated individually, depending on the terrain, nature of the soil and other details. Where appropriate, seedlings are planted. In other locations, seed trees are left in place so that natural reforestation can occur.

The company has close relationships with several nurseries, wherefrom it gathers seeds from trees of a superior quality, processes the seeds, and delivers them to nurseries for germination and development. This enables Santa Fe to acquire a quantity of high-quality seedlings sufficient for its needs at any particular time, without the necessity of maintaining its own nurseries and staff to cultivate the seedlings.

Services and Construction: Leasing and Building

Santa Fe's equipment leasing firm specializes in full-payout equipment leases to leading US corporations, primarily utilities. This equipment ranges from motor vehicles, railcars, computers and corporate aircraft to equipment used in the mining, communication and construction fields. Construction activities are conducted by a major general contractor that constructs office buildings, schools, airports, hospitals and industrial plants throughout the Sun Belt.

Bankers Leasing and Financial Corporation, a Santa Fe subsidiary, is a small organization with only 52 employees. It has a 31-year track record of intense dedication to customer service and rapid response to changes in the leasing business.

It boasts master leasing agreements in place with approximately 150 leading United States corporations, involving about 100,000 pieces of equipment. The equipment under lease ranges from motor vehicles, railcars, computers and corporate aircraft to equipment used in the mining, communication and construction fields. Lease programs are designed by a management team to fit the needs of each individual customer.

Perhaps 85 percent of Bankers' business today, up from 75 percent in 1985, is in leasing equipment to investor-owned utility companies; about one-fourth of those companies in the United States are Bankers clients.

Bankers has grown in revenues and profitability in the hotly competitive leasing business and, at the same time, has maintained its conservative business policies that minimize the company's risks and reward its strengths.

Every asset in the Bankers portfolio is under lease to a high-quality company that has committed itself to lease the asset for a specific period of time. As equipment is retired, new equipment is generally brought under lease to replace it.

During 1986, the uncertainties caused by pending federal tax reform prompted many leasing firms to enter Bankers traditional market area of leasing equipment based on direct economic benefit to the customer, rather than indirect benefits resulting from the investment tax credit and depreciation. In response to this heightened competition, the company restructured its marketing organization, developed new financing products and succeeded in maintaining its strong growth in value of leases outstanding.

Efforts to expand business beyond the traditional electric utility market achieved some notable success when lease agreements were signed in 1986 with several telephone companies. It continues to analyze new opportunities to convince companies that leasing equipment offers major financial advantages compared to purchasing.

The construction industry in the West and Southwest, where SFSP operates, has faced severe problems recently. These problems reflected plunging oil and natural gas prices, previous overbuilding and investor uncertainty due to federal tax reform proposals.

Nevertheless, the company achieved a record $375 million in new contracts awarded in 1986, up 16 percent over 1985. Work completed during 1986 was valued at $282 million. Bad debts and a number of subcontractor bankruptcies, however, reduced or eliminated profit margins on many projects.

Some of the major projects completed or brought under contract as general contractor during 1986 included wastewater and water treatment plants in Houston, Phoenix, Denver and El Paso.

Even with diversification, rail freight is the backbone of the Santa Fe. Such freight transport as the long train *at right* is essential to American commerce: no matter what, freight trains will *see* use.

Among major hospital projects completed or brought under contract during 1986 were the new Woodland Hills Medical Center/Kaiser Permanente in California, and additions to the Methodist Hospital in Houston and the US Naval Outpatient Clinics in San Diego. SFSP is also building additions to several Dallas area hospitals.

Major commercial work under way in 1986 included One Renaissance Square, a high-rise office complex in Phoenix; Preston Commons, a high-rise complex in Dallas; and an eight-story addition to the Hammerson Building in Los Angeles.

One interesting new growth area for SFSP is McKee Products, Inc, a subsidiary that quarries and processes high-grade aggregate for use in transportation and construction industries. A new quarry in California will begin operation in 1987. During 1986 McKee Products began to sell aggregate to non-railroad customers, earning 10 percent of its income from this growth area.

During 1986, the company achieved significant cost reductions by closing construction service offices in Austin and El Paso, and consolidating their functions into its Dallas headquarters. This was made possible by an improved management information system, and resulted in a reduction of staff personnel.

Innovations

Electronics play an ever-increasing role in modern railroading. Computers and a vast communications network have combined to produce dramatic changes in Santa Fe's operations in a few short years. Such things as improved signaling, centralized traffic control, train radio

Besides such projects as the SFSP project *above left*, the Santa Fe has maintained computer-console train routing and composition systems *(above)*, and has given many of their trains the new 'merger' color scheme *(at right)*. Overleaf: An SF triple header near Victorville, CA.

communications, grade crossing predictors, infra-red switch heaters and automatic hotbox detectors result from the application of electronics.

Santa Fe was in the vanguard of the rush toward computerization. Already these electronic marvels have increased efficiency in a number of ways. They handle rapidly and with a minimum of manpower such chores as payroll accounting, car location functions, billing and collections, traffic flow analysis, over-size load routing and simulated train operations.

Santa Fe's microwave network already stretches from Chicago to the West Coast and is constantly being expanded. It is this system that provides direct-dial phone service and the rapid transmission of data to the central computer at Topeka. But even more important is what this sophisticated information gathering and processing system promises. It will enable Santa Fe to better utilize all of its facilities in day-to-day operations. It will provide management with instantaneous data on system-wide operation—information vital to proper advance planning. It foretells a major breakthrough in the science of management.

The track assembly—steel rails spiked to timber ties on crushed stone ballast—is the muscle and bone of the railroad. To the uninitiated it has changed very little over the years. A glimpse behind the scenes, however, reveals that the only constant in the picture is change.

Santa Fe's continuing modernization program sees hills leveled, curves straightened, rivers rebridged, classification yards computerized and highway crossings eliminated. Such large facility improvement projects as these are readily visible.

Less apparent but equally important are the subtle changes being effected in railroads at ground level. The rail itself is heavier and is being installed in continuously welded lengths of 1440 feet to provide a smoother ride and lower maintenance costs. Every component of the track assembly is undergoing constant study and improvement. These changes are, perhaps, less dramatic than a mammoth construction project or a new concept in freight traffic. Nevertheless, they do make an important contribution to increased efficiency.

One major change has been mechanization of track resurfacing and maintenance. Machines designed in the space age have virtually eliminated the pick and shovel. Skilled craftsmen have replaced the 'gandy dancer' of yester year. This combination of men and machines in conjunction with improved techniques insures that the Santa Fe will be 'physically fit' to meet the demand for rail transportation in the future.

It has often been said that the philosophy in the early days of the automobile assembly line was 'give them any color they want, as long as it's black.' A far cry, indeed, from the crowded auto dealer's showroom of today. Dozens of models in every conceivable hue, plus optional accessories, enable a dealer to 'tailor-make' a car to satisfy the needs and desires of a customer.

Much the same as the modern auto dealer, the Santa Fe can and does furnish rail transportation 'tailored' to meet the needs of a shipper. A broad range of specialized cars designed to more efficiently transport freight is available—Auto-veyors, Hi-cube boxcars, Shock Control cars, jumbo covered hoppers and mechanical refrigerator cars—to mention only a few.

New concepts in railroading—piggyback, containerization, unit-trains, high-speed premium service—all are available from Santa Fe. It is literally a shippers' supermarket.

More than rails and freight cars and computers, however, Santa Fe is a body of about 40,000 employees encompassing virtually every skill, trade, craft or profession. The company's progress in its second century depends on these people and those who will join it in succeeding years.

Santa Fe has long emphasized the importance of its human resources. It combs campuses for innovative people—people who realize that what is good enough today will seldom be good enough tomorrow. It seeks people who evidence a capacity for growth. Throughout the organization there are continuous in-company training programs, and Santa Fe provides financial assistance on approved courses designed to improve skills or qualify employees for additional responsibilities.

In short, Santa Fe is fully aware of the need to attract, develop and retain the people it must have to continue to progress—the foundation of future growth and prosperity.

Much the same as in the 1870's, Santa Fe is still seeking settlers—not homesteaders any longer but growth in-

Specialization, diversification—that seems to be the name of the game for the Santa Fe these days. Speaking of the former, the paired diesels *at right* haul a train of specialized SF freight shipment cars.

Above: **A phalanx of Santa Fe EMD SD–40–2 locomotives, comprised of machines that develop 3000hp and are nearly 70 feet long.** *Left:* **With Southwestern mountains in the background, yet another lengthy Santa Fe intermodal freight 'delivers the goods.'** *Right:* **A map of the Santa Fe.**

dustries to locate in the progressive part of the nation served by its lines.

By assisting in the location of these new industries it is continuing to play an important role in the growth of states and cities throughout its territory. All of this contributes to increased payrolls and improved business conditions.

The Santa Fe's industrial development experts provide accurate, up-to-the-minute information about sites, utilities, resources and taxes. They arrange special surveys and provide other assistance to industries seeking new locations for plants or warehouses. The company plans to continue its program for acquisition of land suitable for industrial development and to assist in the development of privately owned industrial parks or districts.

The corporation, which now takes in $5.6 billion per year, says that plans for the future include acceleration of the sale of its fully developed real estate, as well as developing vacant land, like the Mission Bay project in San Francisco.

The Atchison, Topeka & Santa Fe

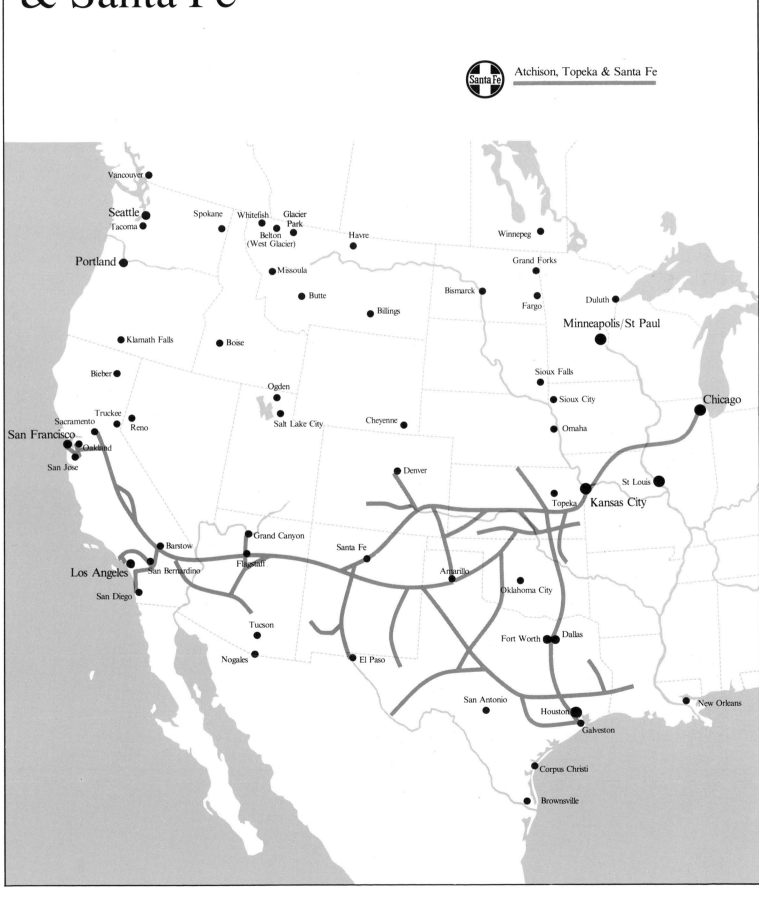

Atchison, Topeka & Santa Fe

Conclusion

The story of the Atchison, Topeka & Santa Fe Railway is really the story of the American West. The railway's early history parallels that of the Old West—just as the rail lines themselves parallel the old Santa Fe Trail—with tales of derring-do, gunfights, desert conquests, prairie settlements, trading of precious goods and expansion across an unknown, sometimes dangerous frontier. The Santa Fe today reflects the fertile, productive New West, a land of agricultural and industrial might. Through the good times and the bad, the Santa Fe has always been there.

It was there when the nation called it to service during two world wars, feeding and moving GIs and sorely needed equipment. It was there during the Jazz Age, reflecting the glamour and wealth of the period with its passenger service fit for kings—and movie stars. It was there when the sometimes cruel forces of nature turned its green territory into a land of dust, providing emergency relief to farmers and cattlemen. It was there again when the region boomed, to ship the fruits of westerners' labors. It is there now, helping to take fuel, foodstuffs and supplies wherever they are needed.

So many men and women associated with the Santa Fe helped to shape American history. Cyrus Holliday played a great part in developing the expansive prairie, both with his individual interest and with his railroad's efforts to settle the fertile land. Fred Harvey, following as he did on the heels of Santa Fe steel, will forever be credited with 'civilizing the West'—and his Harvey Girls and the ranchers they married may in fact be responsible for populating it with young Freds and Harveys! Edward Ripley, who saved the Santa Fe from financial disaster, kept the trains running to towns in need of supplies. Samuel Bledsoe actually kept the railroad profitable during the Depression, saving many jobs, while all around him many businesses went bankrupt.

Not only is the Santa Fe the largest railroad in the United States, it is one of the most enduring. When one looks at the histories of so many railroads, one sees a tangled web of absorption, take-overs and mergers. Not so the Santa Fe. Until its current attempt to team up with Southern Pacific, it has remained a single, strong and steady railroad—since Holliday turned that first spade of earth in Kansas. It will probably stay strong and steady for a long time to come.

At right: **A Santa Fe eastbound freight leaves the tunnel at Tehachapi Loop, near Walong, California. Above it pauses a piggyback; note the intermodal logo on the trailers.** *Below:* **Rolling steady, the Santa Fe.**

Index

These pages: **This photo was taken in the 1950s, when diesels such as these were the fastest thing on rails, and the Santa Fe's Hi-Level cars afforded passengers unmatched views of unparalleled scenery. *Overleaf:* This Sante Fe freight hauls pipeline sections, just as the railroad itself brought forth its own diversified energy interests.**